THE NARRATIVE PATTERN
IN ERNEST HEMINGWAY'S
FICTION

THE NARRATIVE PATTERN IN ERNEST HEMINGWAY'S FICTION

Chaman Nahal

The art of representation bristles with questions the very terms of which are difficult to apply and to appreciate; but whatever makes it arduous makes it, for our refreshment, infinite, causes the practice of it, with experience, to spread round us in a widening, not in a narrowing circle.

—Henry James

Rutherford • Madison • Teaneck
FAIRLEIGH DICKINSON UNIVERSITY PRESS

Library of Congress Catalogue Card Number: 75-131906

Second Printing, 1972

Associated University Presses, Inc.
Cranbury, New Jersey 08512

ISBN: 0-8386-7795-9
Printed in the United States of America

To
my wife,
SUDARSHNA

Contents

Preface   9

Acknowledgments   13

1 Introduction   17

2 *The Sun Also Rises*   28

3 *A Farewell to Arms*   49

4 The Short Stories   80

5 *For Whom the Bell Tolls*   120

6 *Across the River and Into the Trees*   150

7 *The Old Man and the Sea*   170

8 Conclusion   190

Appendix: *Islands in the Stream*   211

Notes   225

Select Bibliography   235

Index   243

Preface

Ernest Hemingway is widely known in India and my interest in him emanates from my school days. However, I began a serious study of him only when I started writing fiction (of a kind) myself and I found him one of those writers, like D. H. Lawrence, Somerset Maugham, Joseph Conrad and James Joyce, whose narrative technique quite impressed me. The present book attempts to give formal shape to what I find to be the most fascinating aspect of Hemingway's art.

A brief paper along the lines explored here was read by me before a conference of American and Indian scholars at the American Studies Research Centre at Hyderabad, India, in 1964. In 1967 came the invitation to visit the United States as a Fulbright lecturer and work at Princeton, and nothing could have been more pleasant, for the opportunity gave me the leisure to write. More than anything else it gave me a close association with Professor Carlos Baker. I would like especially to record my profound gratitude to Carlos Baker for his warm personal kindness and his making available to me his library of Hemingway papers.

In addition to my indebtedness to Carlos Baker, I wish to record my thanks to Mr. G. L. Chandratreya of the Institute of Postgraduate (E) Studies, Delhi; R. B. Magal, Margaret L. Cormack, and W. R. Holmes, all of the United States Educational Foundation in India; Doreen Gee of

9

the Conference Board of Associated Research Councils, Washington, D.C.; Professors A. W. Litz and Lawrance Thompson, and to Mrs. E. J. Miller of the English Department at Princeton; and Dr. W. S. Dix and Miss E. Thomas of the Firestone Library, for their considerate help.

For two years during my stay in the States, from 1968 to 1970, I was also associated with C. W. Post College of Long Island University. My thanks go to Professors Melvin Backman, William A. Fahey, Blossom Feinstein, Dan Levin, Richard Lettis, Yvonne Rodax, S. C. V. Stetner, and Grace Volick, with whom from time to time I exchanged ideas on Hemingway and profited by their comments. I also want to express my appreciation to Mrs. Veronica White, Secretary to the English Department, for her concern for me and for the well-being of my entire family.

For rich, personal friendships, without which our long stay at Princeton would have been meaningless, I owe much to the following: Svetlana Alliluyeva; Sharda and V. Arunasalam; Dorothy and Carlos Baker; Abigail and Nicholas Carnevale; Mrs. Mathilde E. Finch; the late Louis Fischer; President and Mrs. Robert Goheen; Mary and David Hazen; Dennis Jones; Susan and George Mooney; Mary and Robert Prettyman; Dorothy and Datus Smith; and Eleanore and Howard Weed.

The index to this volume was prepared by Dorothy and Datus Smith, and I could not have received more expert help in the matter. Knowing the Smiths was an endless adventure for us, and we found each encounter with them a challenge in the sophistication they brought to bear on life.

My wife, Sudarshna, worked singlehandedly in reading the proofs and checking the quotations from Hemingway.

Her own interest in Hemingway equals mine, and so it was a more than welcome and happy collaboration.

Expenses for typing the manuscript were met in part from a grant made available by C. W. Post College and I thank the school for that. I am also grateful for the financial assistance received from the Conference Board of Associated Research Councils, which administers the Fulbright grant. Not least, I am indebted to Delhi University for granting me leave of absence in order to complete this book.

Chaman Nahal

Delhi University

Acknowledgments

The author wishes to thank the following for permission to quote from copyrighted material:

Mrs. George Bambridge and Doubleday & Co., New York: *Something of Myself* by Rudyard Kipling, Copyright 1937 by Caroline Kipling. Reprinted by permission of Mrs. George Bambridge and Doubleday & Co., Inc.

Mrs. George Bambridge and Macmillan & Co., London: *Something of Myself* by Rudyard Kipling, Copyright 1937 by Caroline Kipling. Reprinted by permission of Mrs. George Bambridge and Macmillan & co.

The Executors of the Ernest Hemingway Estate and Jonathan Cape, Ltd., London, publishers, for permission to quote from *Across the River and Into the Trees, Death in the Afternoon, A Farewell to Arms, For Whom the Bell Tolls, Green Hills of Africa, A Moveable Feast, The Old Man and the Sea, The First 49 Stories, Fiesta (The Sun Also Rises)*, and *To Have and Have Not.*

THE NARRATIVE PATTERN
IN ERNEST HEMINGWAY'S
FICTION

1

Introduction

i

This book concerns itself with Ernest Hemingway's method of telling a story. It also examines the kind of action he is most interested in.

Hemingway was not a systematic critic of the novel, and we do not find him making any deep study either of the genre or of his own novels. Yet, as a working artist, he was surely conscious of the aesthetics of fiction. No artist can function through a medium without, at least by implication, exploring the nature of the medium or the technique of his art. But unlike Henry James, Virginia Woolf, or D. H. Lawrence (to mention some of his contemporaries), Hemingway did not develop an extended theory on the subject.

We can take it that as a novelist his primary obligation was to the structure of his tales. Our concern with "thematic" aspects of a writer often tends to obscure this basic fact. The themes of a writer are important to us. But a writer is essentially a craftsman, a "maker," who puts a few things together. It is therein that his virtuosity as an artist lies. While Hemingway's experiments with prose style have been noted and duly commented upon (as, for example, where Robert Penn Warren likened his accomplishment to the one achieved by Wordsworth in poetic diction in *Lyrical Ballads*), sufficient notice of the structure of his stories has not yet been taken. Hemingway has left us with no detailed analysis of his method, but from his scattered observations in the body of his novels, and in *Death in the Afternoon* and *Green Hills of Africa,* as indeed in some of his published articles, his "nonfiction," it is possible to understand his narrative pattern. His comments are not always explicitly stated, and very often are made in a different context. The possibility therefore has to be exercised with caution.

Almost all academic critics of Hemingway have emphasized the importance he attaches to *action*—"to put down what really happened in action." Carlos Baker is the only critic who, in *Hemingway: The Writer as Artist,* goes deeper and reads symbolic meaning into his work. It is a worthy attempt, for Hemingway's apparent simplicity is most deceptive. Hemingway was a very intense artist, whose diffidence in speaking about his trade, his writing technique, may be ascribed to some kind of shyness or superstition in the man. It was like a magic ritual; the way one built a story. And like any magic ritual, it was supposed to set off a far greater chain reaction, or avalanche, than the simple ritual might imply. As such, all his stories, though on the surface brief and simple, are meant to convey far more than the surface shades of meaning.

But most critics tend to take Hemingway at surface meaning alone. Even his oft-repeated statement, "to put down what really happened in action," has been taken for what it says. None of the critics has questioned Hemingway's own use of his dictum, or has gone on to analyze closely the precise meaning Hemingway put on action.

Most early twentieth-century creative writers were conscious of the limitations of chronological action. It is not certain whether Hemingway was familiar with the critical writings of Virginia Woolf, but in 1919, in her essay "Modern Fiction," she carefully applied herself to some of these problems. Both chronological action and chronological time come in for much censure there. She dismisses the old school of novelists as arranging things a bit too symmetrically. Of her contemporaries, she cites Arnold Bennett, Galsworthy, and H. G. Wells, who still belong to that old school. The new school thinks of life as a more fluid entity. Action and time are spread over a wide range and the chronological sequence is deliberately dislocated. For example of the new school she offers only James Joyce, though she herself was soon to write in the same fashion.

It is doubtful whether Hemingway was influenced by what she said, but in his work he extends the meaning of "action" further than the then new school of psychological novelists. We are making much these days of the anti-novel novel. But in some respects Hemingway was the first novelist to consider the "anti" aspects of a novel. Most of his heroes are anti-heroes, and much of the action in his fiction is really anti-action. In that context, he anticipated Camus and Sartre by many years in some of the techniques that he experimented with.

ii

What is the precise nature of Hemingway's ingenuity in technique? It consists by and large in his taking aesthetic note of moments of passivity as an essential component of any given total action. Awareness of passivity as a norm of behavior is a relatively new concept in Western literature or thought. The entire Western literature revolves around the myth of *action*—of human endeavor; and action or endeavor is equated with perpetual movement.

As far as fiction goes, the only narrative pattern hitherto employed by novelists has been that of uninterrupted movement. It may take the form of what E. M. Forster has called the "then and then" movement, or of a highly sophisticated "stream of consciousness" method as seen in Virginia Woolf and James Joyce. But the essential structure of the picaresque novel and the psychological novel, as should be noticed, is identical. The latter only extends the range of movement to include mental action as well; it does not alter the narrative design. Clarissa Dalloway, for instance, is never at rest, and either her body or her mind is in constant motion. *Mrs. Dalloway* is thereby not much different structurally from *Don Quixote*.

In Conrad and Henry James, again there are various structural novelties. In the prefaces they wrote for their collected works, they discuss their respective methods. Conrad in his novels reviewed the same event from several different points of view, and through a series of flashbacks. The story in *Lord Jim* or *Nostromo* is narrated for us not by a single narrator but by many. On the other hand, Henry James preferred to present a situation through a single controlling intelligence, and the reader's confrontation with reality was always through this central consciousness, never direct. But even in their case, what the novelist is concerned with is a certain stretch of action. What they do is limit the length or duration of that action, and then vary the range of sensibilities that are exposed to that action. Thus, while they undoubtedly extend the scope for characterization and the structural geometry of an action, the movement within that particular piece of narrative is left undisturbed.

It is not until we reach Camus that the concept of

passivity, or stillness, of a cessation of movement is at all acknowledged or recognized in Western literature. Only in Camus's novel *The Stranger* do we see the aesthetic issue posed that something like passivity can be as meaningful in life (and art) as action or activity.

In Hemingway, however, passivity seems to be an integral pillar of his aesthetic framework. He was the first novelist to use inactivity—physical or mental—as part of the structure of a novel. By inactivity it is not implied that all activity comes to an end. What is suggested is a cessation of the action or movement controlled by human will and requiring the individual's conscious participation in it. The result is that for those brief moments when the human will is in abeyance, the individual is driven by forces bigger than himself and which manifest themselves in spite of himself. As far as the individual is concerned, he is at rest; he is making no conscious move, he is "in-active." He has given himself over to these "other" forces in a state of mind indicative of least resistance.

Physical action is thus what Hemingway is in some ways least interested in. There is on the contrary a passivity in him—a creative passivity, for it is a positive force in his novels and not a negative one—which is the complete antithesis of action. Action surely is recorded, but the structural makeup of his novels, the response of his characters, and his own marginal comments register rather the impressive force of inaction which Hemingway imaginatively makes use of to evoke the desired effect in the reader.

That physical action is not Hemingway's principal concern is evident from the distinction he draws between the two kinds of emotion a particular action generates. First there is "the emotion aided by the element of timeliness."[1] Then there is the emotion "which would be as valid in a year or in ten years or, with luck and if you have stated it purely enough, always."[2] This at once puts a premium on the type of action Hemingway is concerned about, for the first has the element of time in it; the second one is timeless. The first, as in journalism, concerns itself with physical action alone, and in reporting that action accurately. But in the second, the artist goes beyond the merely physical. By stating it "purely enough," he brings out the spiritual or the moral tone of the given action.

In a 1935 article in *Esquire*, Hemingway again speaks of "reporting" an action and "making up" an action. He writes: "If you make it up instead of describe it you can make it round and whole and solid and give it life." Then he adds tellingly: "You create it, for good or bad."[3] These are significant observations, for Hemingway accepts here that in the process of creation, of "making up," there comes a point of departure from "put[ting] down what really happened in action." He sees for the artist other involvements than with the merely physical. The artist reshapes the physical either for "good," as he says, or for "bad." The process of "making up" presupposes a departure from the action as one sees it.

Consequently, the weight in the structure of a Hemingway novel emphasizes more the presentation of the emotive effects of a particular action than the action itself. This can be substantiated by a careful perusal of any one of his novels. If we try to isolate the moments of action in each of them, we shall see that such moments do not constitute the vital parts of the narrative. The strength of the story, rather, lies in those pages which take us beyond the physical action to a point of stillness.

We should therefore say that Hemingway is as much concerned with passive action as with active action, and that he tries to present states of consciousness when active action comes to a complete end and passivity takes over. As may be surmised, he projects characters who are willing to submit themselves to this passivity. Thus, we have in him the projection of a passive hero, which is quite in contrast with what is normally believed about the Hemingway hero. His hero will be examined in detail in a subsequent chapter, but we should note that he is an individual who by choice is passive rather than active. In this passivity, he finds a greater fulfillment than in heroic action. In this passivity, he finds a bridge which connects him with the Unknown, with the mysterious rhythm of the cosmos. Creative passivity is thereby the principal canon of Hemingway's conception of art, and we can take note of his narrative pattern only after we have first understood passivity.

iii

How does Hemingway project this passivity through the fabric of his novels and how does he finally build a story? As opposed to the uninterrupted movement that one finds generally in fiction, Hemingway introduces a new concept of "suspended movement." These are not his words, but the conclusion forces itself on one when reading his fiction carefully. Since Hemingway's view of action included both activity and inactivity, he had to present inactivity too as part of the story. To do so, one observes that from time to time he creates a "moment of pause," a kind of caesura, in the narrative, when the onward or forward movement of the story is brought to a halt. It is a moment of vacuum, when nothing is physically happening. Hemingway then employs this moment of pause for a specific artistic use to further the moral design of his story, to register the impact of the conscious action.

It may be argued that such a moment of pause is no different from the analytical approach of the psychological novel, in which the novelist, through a professed exploration of the mind of his characters, tries to achieve the same effect. But that is not true. Analysis, in the sense that analysis is generally introduced in fiction, is used not for communicating impact but for justifying a certain action or a certain character. The line of analysis is to go into the mental mold of a character in order to substantiate his conscious behavior; it is diagnostic in nature. It only supplements the conscious action; it does not depart from it.

But in Hemingway there is absolutely no attempt to justify any action. This, one imagines, was the result of his moral view of life and the aesthetic purpose behind it. A given action has a certain intensity, which vanishes the moment one starts explaining it. Also, any given action has much more to it than what appears on the surface. There are nuances which can only be felt. These nuances also vanish when the process of explanation is brought in.

The attitude in Hemingway seems to be that chance or fate or circumstance confronts a character with a certain situation from which there is no way out. And once the action is over, the character appears to be stunned at the enormity of what has just happened. Using all the artistic resources at his disposal, Hemingway tries to convey the new feeling of shock and recognition that comes over the character after the event. Such a method precludes defensive apologies, for the aim of the artist is not to justify the old but to come to terms with the new, with what was previously nonexistent.

The moment of pause, or caesura, thus marks a total break with the conscious action. Every single novel of his can be seen as composed of two units. The first unit concerns itself with the normal, conventional narrative—the forward movement of action from one event to the other. This unit is a sharp unit of flow. The second unit is the unit of arrest, the unit of relaxation. The forward movement is brought to a complete pause, a full stop. As stated earlier, by the pause it is not implied that nothing happens in the story at that time.

Something is indeed happening all the time, right up to the very last line. Any art has functional limitations, which for the business of communication depends on a medium. In the case of literature the medium happens to be language, which is a somewhat imperfect medium for presenting moments of stillness or pauses because the unit of language, the sentence, is itself dependent for its life on a certain movement, a certain flow in time, from the opening of a sentence to its conclusion. Even as this book is being written, or being read, while we are speaking of stillness in this chapter, we are doing this in the context of movement.

Similarly in Hemingway, by stillness or arrest of the forward movement of action it is not implied that all activity comes to an end. Only what is happening now is happening at a different rhythm, at a different speed. It is like the human heart beat. The heart is functioning all the time, but between the two beats it stops for a while before resuming the next beat. It does not cease to function when it rests between the two beats; it is very much alive. Its muscles relax and its chambers fill themselves with blood. Follows the quick push, the forward flow, and then again the passivity. But the diastolic activity of the heart is as essential a part of its total life as the systolic activity.

In Hemingway there are similarly two modes of action: the systolic, the active action, and the diastolic, the passive action. In the latter—to my mind the more important mode of the two—the movement of the forward action comes to a standstill. Then follows the diastolic period, when the individual returns to a deep mystery within himself through passivity and makes himself ready for the next systolic move. These are not moments of analysis (or self-analysis, if you like) or moments of introspection. These are moments when the individual is in touch with the rhythm of total life, the dark mystery that surrounds man all the time and of which he can only occasionally become aware.

Seen as an artist who uses such rhythmic impetus successfully, Hemingway belongs to the great tradition of American fiction, where the novelists have tried to come to terms with the dark unknown of life. He belongs to the tradition of Hawthorne and Poe and Melville, where darkness has been the major theme. Hemingway has acknowledged his indebtedness to Mark Twain, as far as his style goes. But he is closer in his cosmology to the Hawthorne-Poe-Melville tradition. As with them, his moral awareness springs from his awareness of the larger life of the universe. Compared with the larger life of the universe, the life of the individual is a puny thing, a tragic thing. But in the larger life of the universe, the individual has his place of glory. Hemingway makes us aware of that, time and again. His characters are conscious of their smallness, compared with the larger life of the universe. Hence the moments of *nadas* or pessimism and scenes of restlessness and nights without sleep. But his characters are also aware of their glory, when they have passively subjected themselves to the larger life of the universe. Says Robert Jordan in *For Whom the Bell Tolls*: "And if you stop complaining and asking for what you never will get, you will have a good life. A good life is not measured by any biblical span."[4] Having just consummated his love for Maria, he is passing through a diastolic pause in his consciousness. The forward movement of the story is at an end and there is a definite suspension of the flow of time. And he at once realizes the relationship that exists between him and the rhythm of the universe.

But in Hemingway we go a step further than Hawthorne, Poe, and Melville in our acceptance of the great unknown of life. In them, darkness is treated only thematically; it is symbolized; it is projected on a screen and scrutinized. Usher, Pearl, Hester, Ahab—all are used by their creators to verbalize their concern with darkness. In Hemingway, darkness is approached structurally too. While his characters are just as much concerned with the black mystery of life, he provides occasions structurally for them to be so. The fabric of conscious action is here perforated, and the entire story moves at the two levels—of conscious, systolic action and of passive, diastolic action. This is a significant contribution to the tradition to which Hemingway as a novelist belongs.

2

The Sun Also Rises

i

Hemingway's first novel, *The Sun Also Rises*, was published in 1926. Virginia Woolf's *Mrs. Dalloway* had appeared a year earlier, in 1925. Joyce's *Ulysses* came out in 1922, as well as T. S. Eliot's *The Waste Land*. At home, in the United States, Faulkner's *The Sound and the Fury* was to appear in a few years' time, in 1929. It seems necessary to mention these dates and other titles to show that in the history of English and American literature this was a decade of great experimentation. One could easily refer to the period as the "Complex Twenties," when complexity in literature was forced on the artist by his subject matter. Complexity in structure and design necessarily developed, for the artist found himself incapable of communicating intricate and complex thematic involvements without resorting to a correspondingly involved manner of expression.

William Empson in *Seven Types of Ambiguity* has examined in detail the rise of obscurity in modern literature, particularly in the literature emanating from the complex twenties. It is surprising that in this decade so conscious of the new literature, Hemingway's *The Sun Also Rises* should not have been seen as a work possessing the same kind of complexity. The novel was immediately praised as a major work, and Hemingway's style was approvingly commented on. But most contemporary reviewers took it as a satire, with its meaning all on the surface, as a pungent criticism of the so-called lost generation. Hemingway himself, however, did not see the book as a surface satire. His rebuttal of the lost-generation tag is only too well known by now; on the very page on which he recorded the remarks of Gertrude Stein, he added a quotation from Ecclesiastes rejecting those remarks. He wrote clearly to Maxwell Perkins that he had not conceived of it as a satire but as a tragedy—a tragedy "with the earth abiding for ever as the hero."[1] But in addition to the subtlety of theme, the structure of the novel is equally complex; and as virtuoso also, Hemingway compares favorably with his peers, T. S. Eliot, Faulkner, and Virginia Woolf, the great artists of the complex twenties.

We can appreciate this by first understanding the main action of *The Sun Also Rises*. It concerns a woman who is associated with a number of men, with most of whom at one time or the other she sleeps. The action further concerns a war casualty, a man who, in love with the woman, cannot consummate his love because of physical incapacitation. The forward action of the novel also concerns a bullfighter, who comes late into the story when all the other persons have gathered together in the course of the action.

This is a fairly accurate synopsis of the story, as far as systolic action is concerned. But in none of these channels of direct action can one think of a scene in the novel where the physical action stands out as a major piece of narration. Brett's nymphomania, Jake Barnes's love for Brett seen in terms of actual response in action, and the bullfighting in Spain with Romero in the ring are presented to us only in the fashion "which gives a certain emotion to any account of something that has happened on that day"; they are not treated as if they were "the real thing."[2] Further, we see that what could have been scenes of impressive physical action—Brett's escapade with Cohn, the arrival of the bulls in the ring at Pamplona, or the scene where Cohn beats up Pedro Romero—are reported to us only after they are over; there is no firsthand portrayal of them. It seems certain that whatever else *The Sun Also Rises* may be, it is not a story of great action.

The novel is instead a presentation of emotional complexity—a complexity which may originate in action, systolic action, but which ultimately transcends it and is independent of it. The theme of the novel is, as Hemingway puts it, "the earth abiding for ever," which means that the present set of characters and what happens to them is only a small part of that total drama of life around them. The theme of the novel is cosmos, and specifically, in the context of the story before us, it is the fate of a few characters as placed by the side of that cosmos. At the level of these characters, the theme is one of hopeless love —the love between Jake Barnes and Brett. All episodes are developed from, all events point to and inform, that single emotional fact. Throughout the story there is an unceasing refrain: "With them was Brett. . . . And with them was Brett [Jake]. . . . Oh, darling, I'm so miserable [Brett]. . . . Don't look like that, darling" [Brett to Jake]. Even Brett's involvement with other men serves to set in perspective her total involvement with Jake. For she takes none of the men seriously "except Jake here," as she tells Count Mippipopolous.[3] It is Jake alone about whom she "never jokes." Their love is the leitmotif of the novel.

It is a measure of Hemingway's skill as an artist that he elects to explore an emotional situation that is without redemption. Dickens in *A Tale of Two Cities* and D. H. Lawrence in *Lady Chatterley's Lover* confront us with a similar theme, but the position is saved there by the novelists' reliance on what may be called ideological substitutes. Sydney Carton has the faith that he can at least find his individual fulfillment by sacrificing his life for the sake of Lucie. Connie in *Lady Chatterley's Lover* is married to a man who is physically in the same condition as Jake (and because of a war injury). But she has a few "theories" about love (whispered into her ear by Lawrence), and when Mellors appears on the scene she leaves Sir Clifford without much hesitation. Hence, by imbuing their characters with dogma—derived in the case of Dickens from Victorian complacency and sentimental fervor, and in the case of Lawrence from polemical sexual beliefs—these novelists can with some ease resolve structurally an intricate situation.

Jake and Brett have no convictions, theological or intellectual, to fall back on. At the same time there is no physical fulfillment for them, either. It is thus a story of absolute commitments, with all lines of retreat cut off, and by narrowing the scope for thematic variations, Hemingway poses for himself grave aesthetic problems and makes his task as a novelist harder. But he also succeeds in making his novel a greater work of art. *The Sun Also Rises* is richer than *A Tale of Two Cities* and *Lady Chatterley's Lover* precisely because it is a masterly exploration of a situation beyond hope.

The relationship between Jake Barnes and Brett is the motivating force behind *The Sun Also Rises*, without which the novel loses its validity. Even Brett's affair with

Romero does not take her away from Jake. She obviously gets much satisfaction from the affair:

> Brett was radiant. She was happy. The sun was out and the day was bright.
> "I feel altogether changed," Brett said. "You've no idea, Jake."[4]

But as Carlos Baker points out in *Hemingway: The Writer as Artist*, Brett is Circe, and this radiance is partly the result of the pride of another victory. Also, as Mike correctly surmises, Romero has sharply awakened a dormant, protective instinct in Brett. "Brett's rather cut up," says Mike. "But she loves looking after people. That's how we came to go off together. She was looking after me."[5] (Brett herself gives Jake a similar reason for her romance with Robert Cohn: "I rather thought it would be good for him.")[6] Physically gratifying though her relationship with Romero may be, we can easily see the maternal instinct playing at the back of it and soon coming to the fore. She takes his food to his room, she is worried about the wind on the day of the fight, and her final renunciation of him has similar overtones: she sends him away in a maternal gesture because she thinks it will be good for him. Her cry at the end of the novel, "Oh, Jake, we could have had such a damned good time together,"[7] is her avowal of her supreme awareness that everyone else, not excepting Pedro Romero, was to be sought after only because Jake was not to be there. Some men made her feel like the wicked Circe; others invoked the motherly instinct. Jake alone had touched the woman in her.

Since the story in *The Sun Also Rises* is narrated by Jake in the first person, it is primarily through his responses that the diastolic action is to be seen. When the novel opens on the systolic note, he has already acquired a detached frame of mind and a cultivated aloofness which comes from long-suffering. It does not particularly matter to him with whom or where he spends his time. We do not yet know of his war injury, nor of his love for Brett. But his lengthy sketch of Cohn's character, with whom he has little in common, and his encounter with Cohn and Frances impress on us his indifference to his choice of associates. If withdrawal is an indication of inner poise, Jake has already reached that illumination. For with an amused noninvolvement he goes on to give us a long account of Cohn, who has been connected with him for some time. Cohn and Jake are to clash with each other over Brett, but that will be later. At the moment, Cohn is a boxer, a Jew, and, worst of all, a literary pretender. And yet Jake seems to have compassion enough for him to build him up for us. If the novel had started with Jake's account of Bill Gorton (as Book II of the novel does), that would not have served Hemingway the same artistic purpose—that of revealing Jake's emotional detachment.

Cohn's decision to break with Frances, and his suggestion to Jake that they take a vacation to South America, elicit the following reply from Jake:

"Listen, Robert, going to another country doesn't make any difference. I've tried all that. You can't get away from yourself by moving from one place to another. There's nothing to that."[8]

This answer must be closely marked by us, for it establishes early in the book Jake's aloneness and his ability to live with himself. It not only establishes his aloneness; it also establishes the extent of his moral awareness. "You can't get away from yourself" is another way of saying that one has to learn to face the reality of oneself—have the courage to face that reality—and to face the reality of the total life around one. Going away to South America would not alter that pattern. Jake's remarks also imply that he himself has gone through a similar cycle. "I've tried all that," are the words of a lonely man who has run the gantlet, has gone through hell and purgatory and has now come out at the other end. "I've tried all that," he tells Cohn, almost like a long-suffering saint.

The novel thereby begins on a note of structural experimentation, which sets off the character of the protagonist sharply.[9] Very early we are given a glimpse of the two worlds, that of the self-projected, ego-maintained action of Cohn, and that of the subdued world of passivity, of creative awareness of the totality of existence of Jake Barnes. This pattern establishes itself firmly by the time Book I of the novel is finished, and then it repeats itself through the entire book. There is the world of systolic action, and there is the world of diastolic action. Many characters are involved in the drama that now unfolds itself before us: Jake, Brett, Robert Cohn, Frances Clyne, Mrs. Braddocks, Georgette Leblanc, Zizi, Count Mippipopolous, and some of the characters, particularly Jake and Brett, move freely from one world to the other. Though these worlds function at the same level, they are independent of each other in a striking way.

Our concern with these two worlds, or two types of action, is both qualitative and structural. Unless we see how the diastolic action complements the systolic one, we will lose the meaning of the work. In the forward movement of the story there are breaks, interludes, and pauses which in thought and action are distinct from the main story but which give additional force to the theme and structure of the novel. When Malcolm Cowley in an essay on *The Sun Also Rises* says that "the street-by-street accounts of Jake Barnes's wanderings through Paris"[10] weaken the story, he misses the intent of the novelist. A little consideration would show us that these wanderings are included by Hemingway on purpose, and that they form in the story some of the pauses, the moments of diastolic action. They—the street wanderings—are a mute insistence of Jake's longing, which will not be still; of this longing his physical restlessness and aimless rambles are only an expression. These wanderings help to reveal Jake's character to us, and they add strength to the design of the story.

ii

The systolic action of the novel starts of an evening, when Jake in his ennui wanders from one bar to another. In a dance club he sees Brett with a number of youngsters, and this angers him, for they are an insipid lot. But Jake does not seize the opportunity to do anything about it:

I was very angry. Somehow they always made me angry. I know they are supposed to be amusing, and you should be tolerant, but I wanted to swing on one, any one, anything to shatter that superior, simpering composure. Instead, I walked down the street and had a beer at the bar at the next Bal.[11]

The reaction is typical of Jake, for one nowhere sees Hemingway's heroes acquitting themselves as great men of action (as is generally believed about them). Rather, they are men given over to singular inertia. By inertia, it is not intended to suggest cowardice; it is the quality which has earlier been referred to as creative passivity— passivity by choice. Nowhere in *The Sun Also Rises*, either in his association with Robert Cohn or Romero or Mike, can there be claimed for Jake Barnes the position of a man of action. Even when he is confronted with imminent action, as when Cohn comes forward to hit him, he goes under without offering any fight. The readiness with which he introduces Brett to Romero, a rival, and then leaves them alone that they may go on with their romance, would on the face of it lend credence to Cohn's charge that he is a "pimp." But he does so in conformity with his norm of behavior in the rest of the novel, that of resignation or nonaction. He has been through much, has seen through much, has suffered too much to be really bothered—"I've tried all that." He now wants to be his own self, detached and uninvolved.

The first momentous interruption in the novel, when systolic action ceases and passivity or diastolic action takes over, comes when Jake returns to his room after his evening of booze and meaningless conviviality. He has been alone with Brett for a good while during the evening, and while he was with her the ache of love had made itself felt immediately. But there are no protestations from him when he is with Brett; his self-possession is absolute. He has been making fun of his injury, he has even been acting "big," but now he is alone in his room. For some time he continues the act, or as Dr. Eric Berne would have said, playing the game with himself. With an indifference bordering on callousness, he opens his mail and attends to its contents. The minute details that Hemingway puts into this particular passage—details of Jake's apparent absorption with the world of conscious, systolic action—help to heighten the impact of what Jake has borne through the years. He makes note of his withdrawals from the bank and discovers that he has a balance of $1,832.60. Calmly he writes the figure down on the back of the bank statement. He reads about the forthcoming marriage of Katherine Kirby, and proceeds to make light of the name. He then adds up the list of all the people he knows of who have pompous names or names with a title.

We are now slipping into diastolic action. Systolic action is moving on the surface, but below the surface Jake is contending with the fact that he has spent an evening with Brett after a long time—with Brett for whom he so passionately longs. And then suddenly, while he is making fun of the pompous names and is supposed to be in a hilarious mood, the systolic activity, the activity controlled by the will of man, or conditioned by it, stops, and the forward movement of the story comes to a stop too. We are in the diastolic period now, the period of a pause in the narrative.

We hear Jake saying: "Brett had a title, too. Lady Ashley. To hell with Brett. To hell with you, Lady Ashley."[12]

This sentence comes all of a sudden. The abruptness of the remarks, the compulsive need for them, shows the onset of diastolic action.

Though he still keeps up the brave front and even tells us the colors of the bullfight papers by his bed ("One was orange. The other yellow"), his hold on his conscious mind has slipped in spite of himself. He is now in another level of consciousness. It must be stressed that the other consciousness or the passivity noticed here is not to be confused with the subconscious hold of psychological fiction. The subconscious of psychological fiction is a part of the conscious mind; it supports and controls the conscious mind. The novelist returns to it to substantiate the conscious action of his characters; he goes to it to find support for what is happening on the surface. But the passivity or the other consciousness of Hemingway is a different realm of awareness, which coexists with the conscious mind in its own right.

The human psyche is a very complex thing, and one of the disservices that psychology, at least Freudian psychology, has done mankind is to explain away the human psyche and destroy its mystery and complexity. The entire body of literature, in all ages and in all countries, has concerned itself with the question of moral evil. Why should there be evil in the world, for which there is no logical explanation? We can understand the evil that man brings on himself through his misdeeds. But why should there be collective evil, evil for which the individual is in no way responsible? Psychology never attempts to go beyond the limited nature of its investigations. It never concerns itself either with the totality of life or with the mystery that created life.

There are thus levels of consciousness over which the human mind may have no control. His subconscious he may be able to understand, may even be able to sublimate or rise above. But what to do with the other levels of consciousness?

There are not only other levels of consciousness, there is another level of "time" as well. J. W. Dunne, the noted physicist, mathematically tried to prove the existence of time completely independent of man or his known consciousness or his knowledge. His books, *An Experiment with Time, Intrusions?, Nothing Dies,* and *The Serial Universe,* are known to scholars in the West but are not so widely read as they should be. Dunne was one of the few Western scientists to take formal note of modes of consciousness or time lying outside the conscious range of the psyche. But the time theories of Dunne and the concepts of the unknown time are not magic formulas or formulas dealing with the supernatural. The argument behind these theories is that the human psyche can in its normal state of awareness function only in terms of the known. But there are moments when the unknown can make itself felt to the human psyche. No preparation on the part of the psyche is required to meet the unknown. Preparation, rather, will interfere with the communion with the unknown. This communion comes on its own. The only contribution required from the individual is that he be in a state of passivity, that his conscious ego and will be in abeyance. In such case, the individual becomes receptive to the unknown, he is in a state of readiness to receive the unknown when it visits him.

Jake Barnes is now at that level of passivity, and the forward movement of the story is halted. We are now functioning at a different time level. There is a pause, as far as the conscious time level is concerned. He undresses, looks at his mutilated body, and gets into bed. His head starts "to work." "The old grievance," he mutters:

I never used to realize it, I guess. I try and play it along and just not make trouble for people. Probably I never would have had any trouble if I hadn't run into Brett when they shipped me to England. I suppose she only wanted what she couldn't have. Well, people were that way. To hell with people. The Catholic Church had an awfully good way of handling all that. Good advice, anyway. Not to think about it. Oh, it was swell advice. Try and take it sometime. Try and take it.[13]

This may seem to be rationalizing, but it is not. The whole scene is a part of the tremendous forces that are now making themselves alive and for which he has no apt verbal formulations. The repetitive "Try and take it sometime. Try and take it," with respect to the maxim not to think about the past, is not a call of wisdom but of the hopelessness of such a procedure. The force of Jake's conscious will is down now, and we have Jake before us in the raw—lonesome, miserable, madly in love, and longing for consummation.

And this is what follows:

> I lay awake thinking and my mind jumping around. Then I couldn't keep away from it, and I started to think about Brett and all the rest of it went away. I was thinking about Brett and my mind stopped jumping around and started to go in sort of smooth waves. Then all of a sudden I started to cry. Then after a while it was better and I lay in bed and listened to the heavy trams go by and way down the street, and then I went to sleep.[14]

The rapidity of Jake's emotional shifts, the brevity of his admissions, the horror of the spontaneous tears are recorded by Hemingway with much ability. Contrasted with what has gone before in the novel, the present moment is characterized by immobility. For a while the immobility is shattered when Brett arrives at Jake's flat, drunk and demanding and talking incessantly of her latest lover, Count Mippipopolous, and for a second Jake feels sorry that he should have been crying for such a woman. But this is just for a second, for his passive self is in complete control and his will cannot function yet. He has only to look out of the window at Brett to feel forlorn once again:

> I went back upstairs and from the open window watched Brett walking up the street to the big limousine drawn up to the curb under the arc-light. She got in and it started off. I turned around. On the table was an empty glass and a glass half-full of brandy and soda. I took them both out to the kitchen and poured the half-full glass down the sink.

I turned off the gas in the dining-room, kicked off my slippers sitting on the bed, and got into bed. This was Brett, that I had felt like crying about. Then I thought of her walking up the street and stepping into the car, as I had last seen her, and of course in a little while I felt like hell again. It is awfully easy to be hard-boiled about everything in the daytime, but at night it is another thing.[15]

iii

It is in scenes such as this that Hemingway's original contribution as an artist becomes noteworthy. It should be admitted that most twentieth-century writers—poets, dramatists, or novelists—have looked upon external action as suspect and have attempted to go beyond it to a new understanding of time. Bergson's *durée* has had wide popularity, and Virginia Woolf, T. S. Eliot, James Joyce, and D. H. Lawrence have tried to interpret it in their own way. But instead of going beyond external action or physical time, as *durée* really implies, most of the time they only entangle themselves in a debate on the subject. T. S. Eliot's line "all time is unredeemable" in *Four Quartets* is of special interest, as it is representative of the interpretation most modern writers have put on *durée*.[16] The entire poetry of Eliot revolves around the concept of time, but in *Four Quartets* it is the main theme. Eliot's "all time is unredeemable" suggests that time is a permanent entity or a fixed entity beyond which man cannot go. He shrewdly sees the relationship between the past, present, and future, but he sees it only at the level of the intellect, at the level of the known. But *durée* or spiritual time depends more on human intuition. It is a state of consciousness which transcends the intellect and works with its own secret rhythm.

D. H. Lawrence comes closer than any other of these

artists to Bergson's *durée*. His "mindlessness" is symbolic of the dark forces functioning in the universe and in man, which forces he sees as supreme. But even in his case, at times it is a "discussion" of mindlessness rather than a creative presentation of it. Almost two-thirds of *Women in Love* is over before Rupert Birkin can convince Ursula that it is better to follow the blood than the mind. But in Hemingway we are taken beyond the external action by catching the characters off guard. This may appear ambivalent, for surely those characters are his own creation, as are the moments when they are supposed to be off guard. But in his ability to make the moments when we see his characters without their masks look natural, as if the novelist himself were startled at the secret revelations, lies Hemingway's talent. Writing to Bernard Berenson in 1954, Hemingway described the ability to make the impalpable not only palpable but natural as the chief virtue of an artist.[17] He himself possessed this ability in ample measure.

iv

The day after Jake's encounter with Brett described above, Jake is supposed to meet Brett at 5 o'clock in the evening at Hotel Crillon, but she does not appear there. At the level of systolic action, chapter 6 (where this happens) is the dullest chapter in *The Sun Also Rises*, where nothing of value to further the plot of the novel takes place. We discover that Cohn is perhaps in love with Brett, but any sensitive reader of the book should have known that by now. Then we are given a detailed account of what is happening between Cohn and Frances, which has no essential bearing on the rest of the story. But when Jake returns home, tired and exhausted, there comes a scene of passivity, of diastolic action, of such magnitude that it adds a totally new dimension to the novel.

We are now in chapter 7. Jake is going up the stairs and the concierge tells him that the lady of the previous night, Brett that is, has been in to see him and will call again. Soon afterwards Brett arrives, this time escorted by Count Mippipopolous in person. Jake has had a shower and leaves the Count and Brett, to go into his bedroom to dress. He is feeling "tired and pretty rotten" when Brett joins him in the bedroom.

> "What's the matter, darling? Do you feel rocky?"
> She kissed me coolly on the forehead.
> "Oh, Brett, I love you so much."
> "Darling," she said. Then: "Do you want me to send him away?"[18]

She is of course speaking of Count Mippipopolous, but what is the meaning of the "Then" here? What does it denote a break with or a break away from? What does Jake want? What is it that he cannot receive or accomplish in the presence of Count Mippipopolous? He is not the kind of man who indulges in self-pity, so he wouldn't need this solitude for mere verbal reassurances from Brett. What is it that Brett dreads, rather, longs for and dreads at the same time, every time Jake comes too close to her physically? What is the "hell" that she has referred to more than once so far in the story?

She goes to the next room and sends the Count away.

> She was gone out of the room. I lay face down on the bed. I was having a bad time. I heard them talking but I did not listen. Brett came in and sat on the bed.
> "Poor old darling." She stroked my head.

"What did you say to him?" I was lying with my face away from her. I did not want to see her.

"Sent him for champagne. He loves to go for champagne."

Then later: "Do you feel better, darling? Is the head any better?"

"It's better."

"Lie quiet. He's gone to the other side of town."[19]

Again the mysterious interpolation "Then later." What does it signify? What has happened meanwhile? Why is Jake's head suddenly "better" now? Hemingway has preferred to leave this part of the narration an enigma, for perhaps he was not quite sure in his mind whether to give expression to what he wanted to convey or not. Alternatively, he may not have been sure in advance of the limit to which Jake's privation would take him. But it seems certain that during this scene Jake receives and Brett gives him a perverted sexual satisfaction. Such satisfaction has been the subject of literature earlier. But the solicitude with which Hemingway presents the theme, and also how he projects it more as a necessity of the moment or the circumstance in question than as a variation willfully contrived, speak of his craftsmanship.

For Jake and Brett in *The Sun Also Rises*, their longing for each other is a matter of life and death. By the time we reach the scene under discussion, Hemingway has postulated this for us in categorical emotional references. And now that the forward movement of the story is over, we cannot go any further in that direction. In the stillness of the moment, both Jake and Brett see the uncommon and the unthinkable as their present demand—a demand which comes with an insistence and compels obedience. The simple adverb "then," repeated a little later as "then later," shows the fulfillment of that urge, while the forward action of the novel is at a standstill. Brett must have been

aware of what Jake wants. Maybe they have had recourse
to the practice earlier, or have lived in expectation and
fear of it, for that would explain Brett's nervousness whenever she is alone with Jake. But it is a tragic situation,
with almost the inevitability of fate behind it. They had
not willed it or planned it; with their conscious minds
they may even have fought against it. And yet, there it
comes as a strange command which would take no *nada*
for an answer, and Hemingway with extreme skill conveys to us the reversal of the norm, without being too
explicit or too remote, keeping just the right distance
between himself and the reader.

v

It may be pertinent to point out here that for Hemingway the unknown is not always "holy" or "religious" in
a narrow sense. For one could otherwise question the
validity of an unknown which sends out such commands
as Jake and Brett have just received. In this context, one
has to see the biological realism that pervades Hemingway's work. Throughout, Hemingway seems to have taken
the attitude that the unknown is mysterious and he avoids
any attempt to rationalize about it. Artists like Wordsworth and Emerson, laudable though their theories of
nature were, imposed a human design on the scheme of
nature. Nature or divinity (for that is what they meant
by nature) is not always kind to man. In fact, very often
nature is openly hostile to man and, as Aldous Huxley
said, if Wordsworth had been to the tropics he would
have seen a different face of nature. At times nature
seems kind to man, genial to him; at other times it does
not appear to care for him at all.

What is implied is that divinity has its own ethical

standards which cannot be determined by man in terms of his human language. There is an endless mutation going on in life, and the biology of the moment is as strong an attribute of it as anything else. Again, the unknown, or divinity, is also concerned with total life rather than with the life of one or two individuals. Surely the unknown will visit an individual who is in a state of passivity or readiness for it, but the form in which the visitation will come is unpredictable.

vi

Systolic action picks up once again from this scene of diastolic action between Jake Barnes and Brett. Brett goes away to San Sebastian, and in course of time all the major characters, with the addition of Bill Gorton, collect at Pamplona. It is not here intended to offer an analysis of every scene that follows, but the narrative pattern outlined above maintains itself through the remainder of the novel. Of especial interest, in the remaining part, are chapters 14 and 18 in Book II and the whole of Book III. The only time Jake enjoys conscious action is when he and Bill Gorton are fishing together in the mountains. But most of the time he is at his best in inaction. He is then in touch with strange, mysterious forces, and he is at a point of stillness—at peace with himself. The beauty of the unknown, its terrible beauty if one likes, is that no two moments of passivity are alike. Each brings its own challenge and its own response. Occasionally it appears in moments of drunkenness ("Under the wine I lost the disgusted feeling and was happy"), at other times it comes as an impulse to pray (there is only a single reference to this in the novel, but a touching one). Most often it only demands submission to the inevitable.

The last great diastolic pause in the novel is when everyone has departed from Pamplona and Brett has gone away with the bullfighter and Jake is in San Sebastian (Book III). Soon Jake starts receiving Brett's frantic wires for help and he propels himself into systolic action, but for the time being he is utterly passive. The three days that he spends there in that mood are like the world created anew. He makes no reference during that time to any of his comrades or even to Brett. Life around is fresh and cool. He swims in the bay, watches cycle racing, and almost in slow motion Hemingway makes us aware of the sounds and smells of the small town through Jake's sensibility; he is fully alive to what is happening around him. There is a newness in the air and Jake is only a part of that newness. "It felt as though you could never sink," he says speaking of his swimming in the bay, which is symbolic, because for these three days Jake could not sink in the sea of life either.

Come the telegrams and off he goes to seek Brett. The pattern that Hemingway imposes on the structure of his narrative is the pattern he imposes on the lives of his protagonists. Life as well as art runs in a series of cycles: forward movement and pauses in the structure; activity and passivity in the lives of the characters. Jake is back in the world of action, and Brett once again is sitting next to him in a taxi, whispering, "Oh, Jake, we could have had such a damned good time together," and once again the movement of the taxi pushes her against Jake's body, and the story ends with Jake's reply to Brett, "Yes, isn't it pretty to think so?"[20] But the story does not really end; it has just begun again on another cycle. Are we not familiar with the situation and the words? Has this not happened several times before? Of course it has. Of course the conversation which has started will have to go on.

Will there be other pauses in the story, will there be other moments of diastolic action? Of course there will be. Will Brett once again ask Jake if he is feeling better, after an ominous interruption from the author of "then later"? Maybe she will and maybe she will not. What we can say is that they will again be in touch with the unknown. They will have to wait in humility and listen to its call and obey. The novel has not really finished. The novel goes on. The story has in fact just started.

3

A Farewell To Arms

i

Whereas *The Sun Also Rises* is a study of moral disorder, in *A Farewell to Arms* Hemingway devotes himself to order and harmony. The background of both novels is the First World War, the more so in the second novel, where the systolic action is set right in the midst of it. War itself is a symbol of disorder, but Hemingway is not primarily concerned with the war in either of the novels. He sees war as a pressure, something that impinges on human life. But then there are many other pressures to which man is exposed, pressures that impinge on human life in the same way that war does. The primary concern of the novelist is with human response to these pressures, and not with the pressures themselves. In *The Sun Also Rises*, Hemingway sees this response emerging in the form of a massive disorder. In *A Farewell to Arms* there is again surface disorder, but Hemingway shows how order can be created out of that disorder.

Leslie Fiedler in *Love and Death in the American Novel* speaks of the inability of the typical Hemingway character to love, and hurriedly heaps several censorious observations on the novelist: "much addicted to describing the sex act," "descriptions of the sexual encounter are intentionally brutal," is only "comfortable in dealing with 'men without women.' " He goes on to say that Hemingway's women are just "bitches"; "had Catherine lived, she could only have turned into a bitch."[1]

This is unfair criticism, for it is not based on facts. Hemingway has certainly drawn bitches in his fiction, but he has also drawn women full of nobility. Similarly, there are characters in his fiction who seem incapable of love. On the other hand there are other characters who are extremely lofty in that sentiment.

Frederick Henry and Catherine are two characters of the latter kind, and *A Farewell to Arms* is a great novel of love. As in *The Sun Also Rises,* there is a constant refrain here too: "All I wanted was to see Catherine. The rest of the time I was glad to kill."[2] This is Frederick speaking, giving expression to his longing. In *The Sun Also Rises,* however, it was the refrain of thwarted emotion; here it is that of consummation. The order or the harmony is the harmony of love, which manifests itself in spite of the chaos of war. And this harmony is to be seen at all levels of commitment—of society, of the family, and of "fatherhood." For indeed if there is "farewell" at one level of the plot, at the other there is participation and acceptance.

However, this harmony is once again seen or realized by Hemingway through passivity, and it is diastolic action which registers its impact for us. His heroes derive their sensitivity, their power to suffer (Jake Barnes) or their power to love (Frederick Henry), from the immense repose and quiescence they possess. It is beyond them to function merely at the level of physical or systolic action. At that level they are the least alive. The soul in them, the quality which correlates impressions and images and provokes responses of new feelings, functions only when the systolic action has come to an end. For this purpose the structure of each novel is intricately built and evolved by Hemingway to provide periodical pauses or caesuras in the flow of the narration, when diastolic action reigns supreme. It is in diastolic action that Hemingway's characters display their finest nuances, giving each story its peculiar tone and resonance.

ii

We will first deal with the issue of war, for if Hemingway's motive, or the purpose of his art, was to present "action," there could not have been a better opportunity than this one. The systolic action of the novel begins with a scene of the battlefront; the theme on the surface deals with the subject of war. Hemingway could have continued building up that theme through the novel.

It should be acknowledged that the generation which was immediately exposed to the book perhaps read *A Farewell to Arms* as a great war novel, a novel of "action." Robert Penn Warren speaks of the "heroic self" in Frederick and then refers to the hypnotic force of the book.[3] But to a reader of a succeeding generation, who can think of World War I only vicariously, such personally gratifying sentiments do not come easily. He, on the other hand, observes that Frederick is if anything "unheroic." For such a reader the force of the book lies in other directions.

In this respect, it is interesting to observe that Hemingway's editor, Maxwell Perkins himself, had reservations about *A Farewell to Arms* as a war novel. Another reader of the book, Owen Wister, to whom Perkins submitted the novel for his comments because he had expressed great concern for Hemingway, also had his reservations.

In a long letter to Hemingway on 24 May 1929, Perkins gave expression to these views. He said that up to the

point where Catherine and Lt. Henry reached Switzerland, the two elements of love and war combined perfectly; after that the war was almost forgotten. Owen
Wister, on the other hand, saw the novel only as a love
story.[4] Perkins offered suggestions as to how the war might
be brought back into the story, but Hemingway ignored
those suggestions. (Hemingway had in any case written
to Robert Bridges earlier, on 23 February 1929, that he
was *not* attempting to paint a picture of the sordidness of
war in *A Farewell to Arms*. That, he wrote, had been done
by others many times. Bridges was then editor of *Scribner's
Magazine*, in which the novel was serialized.[5])

With the passage of time, one's reaction to *A Farewell
to Arms* as a war novel becomes further qualified and
marked with reservations. From the very start, we notice
that the story begins on a note of "indistinct" specifica-
tions, contrary to the precise naming of a scene of action.
We are told of "a" house, in "a" village, and we are told
of "many" victories, and of the narrator's sitting with "a"
friend, drinking and celebrating, and "someone's" coming
in and eventually of the narrator's going on leave. The
"indistinct" note continues. Frederick returns from the
leave, and we hear of "many more guns in the country"
and "a few more houses" hit by shell fire, of "a" soldier
sitting on a bench outside the house where Frederick's
quarters are and of "an" ambulance beside the door.

The scene is purposefully vague, as though the novelist's
main concern lay elsewhere. Things, objects, and human
beings are mentioned but not strongly individualized.

In addition, Hemingway clearly establishes the boredom
with which Frederick looks at life around him. Unlike a
man of action, he is not only indifferent to the fighting at
the front, but he is also indifferent to the fate of the
combatants.

He goes on leave and even this fails to revive him. A long passage can bear reproduction in full here, as it gives us an insight into Frederick's personality.

This is the account he renders to himself of what he had done when he was away on leave:

> I had gone to no place where the roads were frozen and hard as iron, where it was clear cold and dry and the snow was dry and powdery and hare-tracks in the snow and the peasants took off their hats and called you Lord and there was good hunting. I had gone to no such place but to the smoke of cafés and nights when the room whirled and you needed to look at the wall to make it stop, nights in bed, drunk, when you knew that that was all there was, and the strange excitement of waking and not knowing who it was with you, and the world all unreal in the dark and so exciting that you must resume again unknowing and not caring in the night, sure that this was all and all and all and not caring. Suddenly to care very much and to sleep to wake with it sometimes morning and all that had been there gone and everything sharp and hard and clear and sometimes a dispute about the cost. Sometimes still pleasant and fond and warm and breakfast and lunch. Sometimes all niceness gone and glad to get out on the street but always another day starting and then another night. I tried to tell about the night and the difference between the night and the day and how the night was better unless the day was very clean and cold and I could not tell it; as I cannot tell it now. But if you have had it you know.[6]

What kind of language is this? The synoptic significance of the passage as a commentary on a man of action is self-evident. A man of action is a person who goes out to face the reality of the moment, whereas, by Frederick's own words, he is trying to submerge himself in antidotes to action—drink, sleep, cheap sex, and the like. The passage, however, explodes Philip Young's "trauma" theory. Though Frederick has not yet received the physical wound, he is already frustrated and sick. "But if you have had it you know." Have had what? Surely not a physical injury; that is to be in the future. The cause for his boredom or sickness perforce must be seen in some other factor. But this passage also explodes the myth of the "heroic" Frederick. Frederick rather is a man disenchanted with the life of action.

The actual scenes of battle in the novel are very few; there are only two major ones, as a matter of fact, where we see Frederick in terms of personal involvement with the war. The first of these lasts for one day, the second for about three.

It is in the first that Frederick receives the wound which figures so conspicuously in subsequent Hemingway criticism. But ironically he receives it while he is sitting quietly in a dugout with four of his companions, eating macaroni and white cheese.

Later, Frederick gives a truthful account of what happened when he was hit, and he is merciless in his banter.

Rinaldi has come to see him in the hospital and tells him that he has been recommended for decoration. "What for?" asks Frederick.

"Because you are gravely wounded. They say if you can prove you did any heroic act you can get the silver. Otherwise it will be the bronze. Tell me exactly what happened. Did you do any heroic act?"

"No," I said. "I was blown up while we were eating cheese."

"Be serious. You must have done something heroic either before or after. Remember carefully."

"I did not."

"Didn't you carry anybody on your back? Gordini says

you carried several people on your back but the medical major at the first post declares it is impossible. He has to sign the proposition for citation."

"I didn't carry anybody. I couldn't move."

"That doesn't matter," said Rinaldi.

He took off his gloves.

"I think we can get you the silver. Didn't you refuse to be medically aided before the others?"

"Not very firmly."[7]

One can understand Rinaldi's warm-heartedness, but there is no internal evidence to show that Frederick was at any time particularly valorous. What further baffles the reader is that Frederick has apparently no feelings about the wound he has received. Whereas he is not brave about it, he is not bitter either. A trauma or injury of the psyche can develop only if the physical injury has reached that level of consciousness. But Frederick is unmindful of the incident in a manner indicative of apathy.

In his second involvement with the battlefront, he fares no better. He is by now in love and would rather extend his stay at the hospital in Milan, where he is under treatment. The news of the war reaches him dimly and he registers nothing beyond casual bits like, "at the front they were advancing on the Carso," "The West front did not sound so good," or "the fighting at the front went very badly."

At last he reaches the front, and before two days are over the order comes to retreat—"We heard that Germans and Austrians had broken through in the north and were coming down the mountain valleys toward Cividale and Udine."[8] Along with the rest, he runs to the rear.

That, so far as Frederick Henry is concerned, is the end of his direct involvement with action. It is true that the immediate desertion is brought about by the brutality of the firing squad he had to face, and in order to save his life the only way out was to run. But we are not given to understand that at any time during his earlier participation he felt deeply disturbed by the war. Nor do we see in him any inner necessity to act; after deserting he makes no effort to return to his unit or get in touch with the right authorities. Soon, in a moment of utter passivity, when he is lying exhausted in the train on the way to Milan to rejoin Catherine, he sees in a flash that war in any case is bad. The illumination comes to him when he is in a diastolic stance, when the systolic action has ceased, and he bids "farewell" to war and action for good. "You were out of it now. You had no more obligation," he tells himself. There is a tone of finality in his farewell, which seals his act of disassociation even at the mental level:

> I was not against them. I was through. I wished them all the luck. There were the good ones, and the brave ones, and the calm ones and the sensible ones, and they deserved it. But it was not my show any more.[9]

iii

If these alone, war and action, were the *raison d'être* of *A Farewell to Arms,* the novel would have to be dismissed as a failure. Opinion in the matter would of course vary, but the novel neither registers an atmosphere of war nor records acts of personal heroism which go to make a great war novel, like *War and Peace* or *All Quiet on the Western Front.*

But the essential theme of the novel, and the essential plot, revolve around the emotion of love. It is a story of love at the time of war, but the war is not presented here as a disruptive factor. For the disruptive effects of the war, we have to go to *The Sun Also Rises*. It seems to be a salient feature of Hemingway's art that the mood registered is invariably contemporaneous with the action. The crippling effects of the war, which turned a whole generation into "lost men" or "hollow men," became apparent only after the war was over, and to have transferred a subsequent mood to an earlier period of action would have amounted to artistic dishonesty. But Hemingway preserves his artistic neutrality faithfully. The war—while the war was going on—was bad since one's friends died in it and one suffered injuries. But it did not prevent one from loving, or from enjoying the beauty of nature, or from drinking and eating, or from being sensitive to the seasons (which figure so conspicuously in *A Farewell to Arms*). If anything, the war aided one in those activities: the frustrations recounted in *A Farewell to Arms* are no more than the normal frustrations of all living; they are not abetted by or swollen because of the war.

But in the principal theme, the love between Frederick and Catherine, Hemingway displays all his versatility and his maturity as an artist, and the novel takes on an unusual dimension. For *A Farewell to Arms* is a unique novel of the peace of love, of its harmony and order, in spite of what several critics have said (Robert Penn Warren: "Chaotic and brutal"[10]). On the surface Frederick is cynical and Catherine neurotic. There are several occasions in the story when the pessimistic mood indicative of universal disorder and rejection is overtly stated. Helen Ferguson tells Frederick, when he asserts that he will never fight with Catherine, "You'll die then. Fight or die. That's what people do."[11] When assured by Frederick that she is too brave and nothing ever happens to the brave, Catherine replies: "They die of course."[12] While rowing on the lake in their flight to Switzerland, Catherine does not care whether or not the oar hits her in the stomach: "If it did, life might be much simpler."[13] When Catherine is suffering in the labor room, Frederick exclaims, "So now they got her in the end. You never get away with anything."[14] Images of death and destruction appear at other places as well and they have been systematically counted and labeled by critics.[15] But the subtle, underlying thread behind all this disorder is a cosmic order and particularly the order of consummated love, which takes shape vividly in spite of the fact that Frederick is a cynic, Catherine a neurotic, Rinaldi a ribald, and Miss Ferguson a puritan. The handicaps only help to set off that order and harmony, and it is in the projection and presentation of the feeling of love—in the language and the structural devices employed by Hemingway—that the force of A Farewell to Arms as a great work of art lies.

And it is here also that the power of passivity as an enormous influence of moral perception and individual dignity is registered. For, as has been observed earlier, passivity serves as a medium of communication between Hemingway's characters and the Unknown. Hemingway celebrates the life of the senses, but there is a sixth sense whose life he glorifies even more than that of the five physical senses. And that is the intuitive sense, the submerged "self" of his characters, which every now and then comes to the surface. It is through this sixth sense that Hemingway's characters establish their relationship with "God" or with spiritual wisdom. Judging by their confirmed egos, by what they assert or do in systolic moods, judging by what their minds developed through will and conscious effort demand, the characters in A Farewell to Arms do not appear to be mutually compatible. But in moments of passivity, in diastolic moods—for which Hem-

ingway provides occasions and space through caesuras—
when the ego is temporarily suspended, the intuitive part
of each character takes over. And this intuitive part,
motivated as it is by the moral and final ends of man,
directs the characters to creative and cosmic ends, to ends
of fulfillment, of companionship, of love, in short, to
ends of eternal order and meaningfulness.

Let us consider the growth of the relationship between
Frederick and Catherine. Frederick has hardly any feelings for the girl when he meets her for the first time. He
pursues her, more as though he were following up an
affair than anything else. At the slightest protestation of
endearment on the part of Catherine or at the slightest
demand of attachment from her, his immediate response
is: "What the hell." His sole desire in these earlier en-
counters is to get Catherine into a quiet corner to satisfy
his lust: "Isn't there anywhere we can go?"[16] If Catherine
demurs, he is willing to offer her reassurances of his love,
but confiding at the same to the reader that what he is
saying is a "lie."

> I thought she was probably a little crazy. It was all right
> if she was. I did not care what I was getting into. This was
> better than going every evening to the house for officers
> where the girls climbed all over you and put your cap on
> backward as a sign of affection between their trips upstairs
> with brother officers. I knew I did not love Catherine Barkley
> nor had any idea of loving her. This was a game, like bridge,
> in which you said things instead of playing cards. Like
> bridge you had to pretend you were playing for money or
> playing for some stakes. Nobody had mentioned what the
> stakes were. It was all right with me.[17]

So that is how it is, in the beginning. He is devastating
in his comments and seems to be very sure of himself—

sure of what he wants from life. But his cynicism makes it all the more possible for us to realize the value of the love that ultimately manifests itself for him. He never completely submits himself to Catherine, even then. But he is aware later of the fine thing that has come to pass between them, a rare thing, and to that visitation he does submit.

As far as Catherine is concerned, she is a most sensitively drawn character, a rather unusual character in Western fiction. She is fair and beautiful, which is understandable. Western fiction is replete with fair and beautiful women. But she is at the same time elusive and otherworldly, far too resilient and far too moral to offer scope to an artist for precise formulations and definitions. The unity of form that distinguishes Western art from Eastern is largely based on a cognizable set of values and a correspondingly exact sense of line and form. The artist in the East as well is concerned with values and with line and form, but his objective there is to also suggest forces which the artist, being himself physical in origin and hence limited, can never encompass. Thus most representations in Eastern art tend to be somewhat loose and fluid. This looseness imposes its own unity on the total design of the work, as witness the innumerable frescoes in the Ajanta caves or the unhurried love story of Shakuntala and Dushyant in Kalidasa's play *Shakuntala*. But that kind of unity is different from the empirical unity of Western art.

Catherine is a character painted at the level of the "supra-consciousness" of Eastern art, for she certainly is innocence incarnate in this imperfect and incomplete world. If she dies at the end, it is not because Hemingway was incapable of showing love or because his male characters, as Leslie Fiedler would have us believe, are in-

capable of fatherhood, incapable of bearing the respon-
sibility of marriage. The evidence from the story does not
warrant such a conclusion. Indeed, if she must die, it is
because she is too innocent, too good to live. She is like
Cordelia, another fine portrayal of unmitigated innocence.
With the outline of form and character clearly defined in
the case of most characters in Western fiction, Catherine's
(and Cordelia's) plasticity offers the reader a pleasant
surprise.

That she is no fool and that she is not treating her
friendship with Frederick as an escape from her memories
of her dead lover may be seen from this passage:

> "This is a rotten game we play, isn't it?"
> "What game?"
> "Don't be dull."
> "I'm not, on purpose."
> "You're a nice boy," she said. "And you play it as well as
> you know how. But it's a rotten game."
> "Do you always know what people think?"
> "Not always. But I do with you. You don't have to pretend
> you love me. That's over for the evening. Is there anything
> you'd like to talk about?"
> "But I do love you."
> "Please let's not lie when we don't have to. I had a very
> fine little show and I'm all right now. You see I'm not mad
> and I'm not gone off. It's only a little sometimes."[18]

When one is sensitively aware of what he is doing, of
the "game" he is playing, it ceases to be a game. Catherine
was apparently hit hard by the loss of her lover. But that
event did not destroy her vulnerability to the new. Brett
in *The Sun Also Rises* is not only dead mentally; to a considerable extent she is dead spiritually too. Her whole life
consists in multiplying of experiences in the attempt to

revive a feeling she had once known with someone, then lost. When her lover died in the war, she hung on to the memory of that experience. The lovers that she picks up now, the sexual excesses to which she drives herself, are only somehow to revive in herself the old experience. Psychologists make much of trauma as the impact of an external experience on an individual, which takes hold of his mind for good. But in the ensuing tragedy the villain is not the experience but the individual. Experiences come and go, in their own designated time. But some persons will hold on to a particular experience, even when the experience itself is dead. The variety of life is endless, each day offering something new to those who will be humble enough to receive it. But persons who come to the new with their minds tied up with the past are fundamentally incapable of receiving the divinity of the "new." Brett in her nymphomania is a typical example of what D. H. Lawrence called the "unliving,"[19] for her whole personality is tied up with the dead. Jake alone could have got her to shake off the past, but he was physically incapable of carrying the relationship to that consummation, and hence her attachment to the past remains.

Catherine has no such wish to repeat her past, and it would be unfair to say that she merely uses Frederick to relive her love for her former boy friend. Her love for Frederick is for her as valuable in its own right as her earlier attachment. The completeness of her love for Frederick lies in the fact that it obliterates all that has gone before in her life.

iv

All this becomes apparent to the reader very slowly. The systolic action indicates a spirit of noninvolvement, not only at the level of war but also at the level of love.

But below the surface many things are happening, which are brought home to us by Hemingway with much virtuosity. As we proceed, and as more and more instances of diastolic action are placed before us, we discover that at the level of war a total repudiation takes place (chapter 32). And at the level of love there comes a total acceptance. Chapter 7 in Book I gives us an indication of the change that is to come. By the time we reach Book II, the new import has broken loose like a river.

This particular chapter—chapter 7 in Book I—is a pertinent illustration of the caesura, the break in the forward movement, in the systolic action of the story, planted deliberately by the artist. The systolic action of the story undergoes a transformation here. In the pause that follows, the tone, the images, the physical and mental responses of the character or characters involved all become more pronounced in their openness. Perhaps the character has hitherto been wearing a mask. If so, the mask drops here and one sees his true face.

Until this time, until chapter 7, the story is built on the understanding that there is no love between Catherine and Frederick Henry. The fatal meeting, when each says unkind things to the other, has just ended, and with its end the last hope of any attachment between them. At least Frederick, we know, has no intention of getting involved with Catherine.

It is in the clearly established direction of systolic action that the artistic merit and meaning of the caesura or the pause lies. Hemingway first establishes the systolic mood firmly before switching over to diastolic action. Up to the beginning of chapter 7, the unmistakable development is that nothing more than a casual affair is taking place between the two major characters of the story.

But now Frederick is alone in his room and is in a passive mood. An offensive is to start at the front in a few days, and he cynically tells himself that the Allies have no big general, no Napoleon, to confront the Austrians with. For a second he feels concerned about his safety and wonders if he would not have been better off with a British regiment. And then, as if by a flash, the realization comes to him that he had nothing to do with the war anyway. "It did not have anything to do with me. It seemed no more dangerous to me myself than war in the movies."[20]

The observation is unwished for, and it comes to him at a time when he is least expecting it. But the question here is not so much his noninvolvement with war as the introduction of a different kind of rhythm in the movement of the story. From noninvolvement with war, Frederick drifts into challenges of life which really excite him. One of such recent challenges is Catherine. On the surface he had been trying to suppress his longing for her, or credit it as no more than a casual relationship. He sees now that she means more to him than he had thought. In the long passage that follows, in which he daydreams of spending a night with her in Milan, the essential note is one of tenderness. "After supper I would go and see Catherine Barkley. I wish she were here now." That is how it begins, and if we compare this passage with the one where Frederick speaks of his sexual adventures while on leave, the different tone is immediately noticeable.

> I would like to eat at the Cova and then walk down the Via Manzoni in the hot evening and cross over and turn off along the canal and go to the hotel with Catherine Barkley.[21]

Notice the leisurely pace of the thought and of the sentence. The "hot" evening is symbolic not only of sensuality, but of satisfaction and submission. The unhurried progression toward the hotel, the "walking down," the "crossing over," the "turning off"—all this is in sharp contrast to the "whirling" of his earlier acquaintance with passion ("when the room whirled and you needed to look at the wall to make it stop, nights in bed, drunk . . .").

He is not sure whether Catherine will agree to go with him or not. He keeps up the hope that "maybe she would." The mental picture of their going up in the elevator to the hotel room may seem an erotic fantasy, and to some extent it is. The image still is one of taking Catherine into a room and sleeping with her, as it was earlier of taking her into a quiet corner. But what impresses the reader is the tenderness in the present passage. Even if it is an erotic fantasy, it is a fantasy working at a much higher level than the mere carnal. We hear almost every single sound, every step taken, as a separate emotion to be cared for and longed for. The sexual part of the act is pushed out of the way and what is more pertinent is the physical peace of the moment

> . . . and then we would get in the elevator and it would go up very slowly clicking at all the floors and then our floor and the boy would open the door and stand there and she would step out and I would step out and we would walk down the hall and I would put the key in the door and open it and go in and then take down the telephone and ask them to send a bottle of capri bianca in a silver bucket full of ice and you would hear the ice against the pail coming down the corridor and the boy would knock and I would say leave it outside the door please.[22]

In this sentence, most of the things referred to, and savored, are "non-sexual," if one may put it that way, to bring out the force of the diastolic action. Without his ever consciously planning it, a new self has arisen in

Frederick Henry, where an immense awareness not only of the delight of physical passion but also of the processes that lead up to it is an integral part of that "new" self. He has, as it were, become conscious for the first time of a sense of beauty. Earlier, all that his mind recorded was "nights in bed, drunk, when you knew that that was all there was." Now it comes to him that maybe there are other things to it, too—particularly beauty. "Now beauty, as we said, shone bright amidst these visions, and in this world below we apprehend it through the clearest of our senses, clear and resplendent." So says Plato in *Phaedrus*. Something close to *anamnesis* takes place in Frederick Henry during this first pause in the story, the first assertion of the diastolic action. In place of the earlier gross wants, we have much finer desires now. The sensuous images of sound and sight—of the elevator going up, of the unhurried steps toward the place of destiny ("she would step out and I would step out and we would walk down the hall"), of the key turning in the lock of the door, of the noise of the ice in the silver bucket—are evoked with much delicacy, as if the end desire were not in itself of much value compared with the separate delight of each moment leading up to the last.

The diastolic action is not to be compared by us with any miraculous confrontation, ingeniously contrived by the novelist to bring about a sudden modification in his characters. It is not my intention to suggest that, and such scenes are not to be confused with quick conversions. What is suggested is that the diastolic action takes the character (and the reader) closer to the dark life of the cosmos, and thus reveals to him several unknown possibilities of life, almost all of them somehow associated with beauty. It is not expressly stated in the passage we are examining, but Frederick now certainly seems to see much more in Catherine than merely a woman with a body. At the end of the chapter, when Helen Ferguson turns Frederick away and he cannot meet Catherine as she is unwell, his reaction is:

> I went out the door and suddenly I felt lonely and empty. I had treated seeing Catherine very lightly, I had gotten somewhat drunk and had nearly forgotten to come but when I could not see her there I was feeling lonely and hollow.[23]

The word "lonely" one can understand, but not the words "empty" and "hollow." Frederick has never used such words in this way before. Later, much later, when he sees Catherine in the hospital at Milan, he is to say: "God knows I had not wanted to fall in love with her. I had not wanted to fall in love with any one. But God knows I had and I lay on the bed in the room of the hospital in Milan and all sorts of things went through my head." But the first realization of this love comes to him in chapter 7, where the structure of the entire chapter—the speed of the narration, the texture of the emotions, the linguistic embellishments—all simultaneously focus the reader's attention on that new awareness. And Frederick is, at the moment of that awareness, in a diastolic stance, in a state of utter passivity, open to the new, receptive to the non-active elements of his psyche.

The quality of the love projected between Catherine and Frederick is so rare, so tender, that Hemingway does not attempt once to define that love. "Catherine Barkley took three nights off night duty and then she came back on again. It was as though we met again after each of us had been away on a long journey."[24] It is through references such as this, and through assertions of the newness of their passion each time they come together, that one is made conscious of how deep the involvement is. But Hemingway makes no attempt to define it for us explicitly.

Not only that. One has also to see the finesse with which he projects a sexual union, when such a scene is necessary to the story. Instead of such scenes being "intentionally brutal," as Leslie Fiedler would have us believe, we are given only a hint of the actual sexual act. It is a semi-mystical ritual, which the characters involved alone can understand. And so the novelist makes a reference to it, and then introduces the pause—Hemingway's most powerful technical device to suggest activity beyond the scope of rational comprehension. Thereby, in most of his fiction, the sexual union is the point of departure from the limited experience of the senses to the enormous, mystical experience beyond the senses, and it is seen by Hemingway as belonging more to the diastolic mood. One is led up to it in the systolic fashion, but the actual consummation takes place in the diastolic period.

Catherine Barkley and Frederick Henry are reunited, after Frederick is wounded and sent to a hospital in Milan, where Catherine is also posted. She is in his room, alone. This is their first meeting, after a separation of several weeks. "When I saw her I was in love with her. Everything turned over inside of me." While he had been at the front, or after the injury when he was in the hospital, the inner mutation had slowly been taking place and his spontaneous reaction on seeing her is his acceptance of his love for her. Frederick goes on to take the girl, rather in a hurry, but we must watch the presentation:

> "You mustn't," she said. "You're not well enough."
> "Yes, I am. Come on."
> "No. You're not strong enough."
> "Yes. I am. Yes. Please."

"You do love me?"

"I really love you. I'm crazy about you. Come on please."

"Feel our hearts beating."

"I don't care about our hearts. I want you. I'm just mad about you."

"You really love me?"

"Don't keep on saying that. Come on. Please. Please, Catherine."

"All right but only for a minute."

"All right," I said. "Shut the door."

"You can't. You shouldn't."

"Come on. Don't talk. Please come on."[25]

Up to this, it is all in the systolic vein; the action is moving forward, the demand insistent. But no further description follows. Instead there is a huge pause in the story, which is even typographically indicated—a more than usual space is left before the next paragraph begins.

When the story is resumed, we see Catherine sitting in a chair by the bed. "The door was open into the hall. The wildness was gone and I felt finer than I had ever felt." This may be only the feeling of physical relief. That the consummation has also left indelible marks on his psyche becomes apparent, however, as the novel proceeds.

But the manner in which Catherine asks him "Now do you believe I love you?"[26] is reminiscent of Brett's rhetorical question to Jake Barnes in the bedroom scene, when the two were left alone by Count Mippipopolous. This is how the narration goes there: "Then later: 'Do you feel better, darling? Is the head any better?'" The break in the systolic action, the pause, the suspension of the movement is too obvious in both instances. It is this identical manner of presentation which makes one suspicious that some kind of sexual relationship does take place between Jake and Brett when Count Mippipopolous goes to get the wine. The purpose the adverb "then" serves in *The Sun Also Rises* is served in *A Farewell to Arms* by the adverb "now" and by an equally ruminative interrogatory sentence: "Now do you believe I love you?" The same type of technical device is employed by Hemingway in both places to make the reader aware of the sexual participation. The novelist brings his own narrative to a stop for all practical purposes and withdraws from the scene, leaving the characters in a state of completion of which they alone can be conscious and of which the reader will learn later, by reflex action.

After the scene in the hospital room, Book II of *A Farewell to Arms*, especially chapters 16 to 21, acquires a distinct rhythm, different from the rhythm so far. These six chapters deal with diastolic action, and represent passivity and withdrawal, as far as the will of man is concerned, as far as his ego is concerned. Briefly, they are the chapters of the stillness of love. It is that stage of love where possessiveness comes to assume the least important part of the relationship, and physical passion becomes only a minor part of the total commitment.

Consider a passage like this:

When she came upstairs it was as though she had been away on a long trip and I went along the hall with her on the crutches and carried the basins and waited outside the doors, or went in with her; it depending on whether they were friends of ours or not, and when she had done all there was to be done we sat out on the balcony outside my room. Afterward I went to bed and when they were all asleep and she was sure they would not call she came in. I loved to take her hair down and she sat on the bed and kept very still, except suddenly she would dip down to kiss me while I was doing it, and I would take out the pins and lay them on the sheet and it would be loose and I would watch her while she kept very still and then take out the last two pins and it would all come down and she would drop her head and we would both be inside of it, and it was the feeling of inside a tent or behind a falls.[27]

There is not a single word in the passage to suggest passion. "It was lovely in the nights and if we could only touch each other we were happy." All movement, all demands are come to an end and what they seek now is the point of stillness. In *The Waste Land,* T. S. Eliot closes the poem with the Indian exhortation of "Shantih, shantih, shantih," which, as he correctly translates, means peace that surpasses understanding. A similar peace descends on Catherine and Frederick at this stage. It is a state of contentment that comes rarely in life, and it is even more rare to see it rendered in art. For conventional dialectics cannot face the challenge of this experience; nor can conventional language. Language and opinions tend to revolve around the known, around something that is already within the grasp of the human mind, in short, around the past. But consummation in love is like meeting the unknown; it comes to one as a grace, or as a gift from the divine, and is very close to the religious experience of the saint or the mystic. And just as the experience of the saint or the mystic cannot be rendered in words or be communicated directly, so the experience of love escapes precise formulation.

In most of his fiction, Hemingway slowly takes us to an equally intense "religious" experience. The "religiosity" is not of the conventional type; it is not the quest of man for a personal God. Rather, the religiosity is in what suddenly confronts man in life in a certain intensity. It may be the birth of a child, it may be a tiger hunt, it may be a safari, but slowly Hemingway produces in it a measure of intensity which, though human in origin, carries with it a spiritual impact.

In *A Farewell to Arms*, the locale of the story slowly shifts to a small, single room, where Frederick is lodged in the hospital. In Tolstoy's story "How Much Land a Man Needs," the novelist specified the short length of "three arshíns"—the grave in which a man must lie after his death. For Hemingway the requirements are slightly longer and wider, but they do not exceed the four walls of a room in which a man lives. It is surprising how important a part a "room" plays in Hemingway mythology, for the climactic scenes of his fiction are very often played indoors rather than out of doors; if it is not a room it may be an Indian's hut, or a tent, or any other enclosed place.

Jake Barnes's illuminations come to him in his room, as indeed do those of Frederick Henry. The happiest moments of Robert Jordan, in *For Whom the Bell Tolls*, are those when he is alone with Maria in his sleeping-bag. The experiences of Nick Adams in "Indian Camp" begin inside a shack. The drama of "The Killers" is played indoors.

The outside world in *A Farewell to Arms* slowly shrinks away and falls into the background and the paradise is regained in the confines of one's private habitation. In *The Sun Also Rises*, Jake Barnes's wanderings through the streets of Paris were a clever device used to show Jake's frustrations in love. In *A Farewell to Arms*, since the purpose is to show fulfillment, there is not a single scene of street-wandering until the day Frederick has to leave Catherine behind in Milan and catch the train back to the front. (And on that day, as though to mark the end of their happiness together, Frederick and Catherine walk and walk and walk until Catherine is able to say, "I feel better now . . . I felt terrible when we started.")[28]

Even in Catherine's paranoia, one notices, there comes a subtle, meaningful change as the systolic action comes to a halt in Book II and the diastolic action begins. When we meet Catherine for the first time in Book I, we observe that she is somewhat neurotic. The explanation is not long in coming; she is so because she has lost her lover in the war. But if we compare the long passage in chapter 16, for instance, beginning with her words to Frederick, "Tell me. How many people have you ever loved?"[29] with what Catherine says in chapter 6, beginning with "And you do love me?",[30] it becomes clear that what was previously perhaps a measure of escape for her has now become a measure of life. She is equally frenzied in both passages, but in the one that comes later, in chapter 16, her neurotic state is an effective medium of self-expression. Earlier, her attachment to Henry was perhaps to help herself forget her dead lover. Now it is a measure of her complete identification with the new man. "I want what you want. There isn't any me any more. Just what you want."[31] This she repeats several times later in the story, particularly in the effective lines: "There isn't any me. I'm you. Don't make up a separate me."[32]

Frederick's commitment is equally absolute now, and again Hemingway resorts to effective artistic devices to make us aware of that. Though at one stage Frederick announces, "I suppose I enjoyed not being married,"[35] he slowly assumes the role of a married man and behaves like one. Hemingway's genius is to be seen in the fact that what he urgently wishes to convey to us is never posed in conceptual terms. There are no dialogues or digressions on the subject of love. Hemingway's convictions and attitudes are rendered through delicate change and transformation in the characters themselves, of which change they may not only be not aware but which they may even openly disown. And so, quite theatrically, Frederick tries to tell himself, "I suppose I enjoyed not being married." But when he returns to the front, the change in his personality, the change brought about by his association with Catherine, is so obvious that the first thing Rinaldi says to him is: "You act like a married man."[34]

It is in this creative transformation, in the metamorphosis that comes to take place in the individual, that the power of diastolic action is to be judged. Through repeated journeys into the unknown, through repeated diastolic pauses, all partial commitments become absolute. Eventually, we know, Frederick deserts from the army and he and Catherine start living together. We are now in Book IV, and the attention of each is focused on the other. Beginning with chapter 34, the tenderness of their love is made apparent to us through repeated caesuras, filled with passages of extreme diastolic beauty and sensitivity. There is a feeling of "arrival" in the air, and it looks as if Frederick's and Catherine's separate selves have dissolved for the time being.

After his desertion from the army Frederick meets Catherine, and their first night in the hotel is for them as if they "had come home." Frederick at least, realizes that "all other things were unreal;" the only reality for him is Catherine. We have known earlier of Frederick's fear of loneliness. We have his own words that when he was on leave he had to drug himself with drink to go to bed. But after the touch of the diastolic reality, that fear is changed into confidence. With Catherine, he never needs an escape—of drink, or of repeated physical abuse.

> We slept when we were tired and if we woke the other one woke too so one was not alone. Often a man wishes to be alone and a girl wishes to be alone too and if they love each

other they are jealous of that in each other, but I can truly say we never felt that. We could feel alone when we were together, alone against the others. It has only happened to me like that once. I have been alone while I was with many girls and that is the way that you can be most lonely. But we were never lonely and never afraid when we were together. I know that the night is not the same as the day: that all things are different, that the things of the night cannot be explained in the day, because they do not then exist, and the night can be a dreadful time for lonely people once their loneliness has started. But with Catherine there was almost no difference in the night except that it was an even better time.[35]

We must compare this passage as well with the one quoted earlier, where Frederick speaks of the night in different terms, to assess the transmutation that Catherine has brought about in Frederick and the method Hemingway employs to suggest an emotional situation to his readers. Catherine and Frederick both are different persons at the end of the story from what they were in the beginning; they are so new that they are almost indistinguishable and we appear to be meeting them for the first time. Catherine's hysteria and Frederick's cynicism are transformed from instruments of denial to instruments of assertion and faith. "Nights in bed, drunk, when you knew that that was all there was, and the strange excitement of waking and not knowing who it was with you" of the beginning is now mutated to an organic and creative experience where the nights are even better and more peaceful than any other time, for "you" are with someone you cherish—or rather both that person and you are in touch with a power bigger and greater than everything else, the power which gives and withdraws graces and which, at the moment, is closely in touch with you.

Count Greffi asks Frederick, "What do you value most?" and Frederick unflinchingly answers: "Some one I love."[36] He tells us he is "faint" with loving Catherine so much. He tells us that the religious feeling comes to him only when he is with her. When they reach Switzerland after the long row over the lake, what touches him is not that they have reached safety but that they have reached safety "together."[37] A few days before their baby is due, he confides to Catherine, "I'm no good when you're not there."[38] When Catherine announces her desire to keep herself beautiful for his sake so that he might fall in love with her over and over again, he replies: "I love you enough now. What do you want to do? Ruin me?" Follows:

> "Yes, I want to ruin you."
> "Good," I said. "That's what I want too."[39]

Also, it should be noticed that, in the comparison between the day time and the night time suggested in the passage quoted above, Hemingway is conscious of the two time factors. In the night time, he seems to make a further distinction between the false night and the true night. "Things of the night cannot be explained in the day, because they do not then exist."[40] That is what sets off the distinction between the two modes of time. He then makes Frederick say: "The night can be a dreadful time for lonely people once their loneliness has started." In several of Hemingway's short stories, as we will see later, the narrator cannot go to sleep, indicating once again a different kind of rhythm encountered at night. He, the narrator, cannot go to sleep when he remains only at the level of the false night, which is in fact not a different time mode but merely a repetition of the day.

He keeps awake, because he is not letting the night take over; his mind can function only in the context of the day, and the day comes and haunts him in the form of memories.

But there is the other night—the "true" night. In the last chapter, an attempt was made to place Hemingway in the Hawthorne-Poe-Melville tradition. It seems certain now that if we are to place Hemingway in the living, or what F. R. Leavis would have called the great, tradition of American fiction, it will have to be in the tradition that has taken willing note of the darkness that surrounds man and all created life from birth to death. For Hawthorne, the darkness meant a social evil. For Poe, it was merely a device to create the right atmosphere. For Melville, it meant mystery, but it remained beyond the reach of and even hostile to man. In Hemingway the darkness implies the functioning of the individual at a different time level. True darkness is man's glimpse of the unknown; true night is a revelation to him of the "other." That is why Frederick can say, "But with Catherine there was almost no difference in the night except that it was an even better time."[41] True darkness or true night is man's existence in the diastolic rhythm.

The finale of the novel, where Catherine dies in childbirth, is most moving and is shattering in its impact. Why should she have to die? Was Hemingway trying to present through her death a rejection of human love, as several critics have stated? Is she snuffed out merely to offer Frederick his freedom afresh?

The only way we can find some meaning in it is by putting forward the hypothesis that Hemingway in this novel is trying to suggest two different environments: immediate and ultimate. Hemingway's pessimism is pitched not against the immediates but against the ultimates. At the level of the immediates, life is happy and gracious; only at the level of the ultimates does it rise larger than the individual and appear to beat him down. Catherine's death thus presents not the death of love but the victory of the ultimates. "So now they got her in the end."[42] "They just keep it up till they break you"[43] (Catherine). "Stay around and they would kill you."[44] The mythical "they" are the cosmic forces, the ultimates. But these "they" are not against man as such. They are against no one as such. What is implied by Hemingway is that the universe has its own rhythm and man is but a small part of its totality of motion. Ultimately, if the artist is to celebrate life—as he must, for *that* is his business as an artist—he has to celebrate the glory of the larger life of the universe rather than of the little creature called man, who is only a minor functionary in that total makeup. It is a pity indeed that Hemingway never formulated his aesthetics, for assuredly he is offering something radically new in this concept of reality. For the most part, artists have celebrated the glory of man. In Hemingway, however, the artist celebrates the glory of the cosmos. ("The earth abideth forever.") His mimesis or imitation is not solely an imitation of the life of man, but of the larger life of the universe. This—the diastolic rhythm of the universe (as opposed to the systolic rhythm of man)—is what Hemingway tried to portray in his major novels. Only with his last novel, The Old Man and the Sea, does the complete picture of man in the context of the cosmos emerge in his fiction. But in the earlier works too the attempt is made to present that total texture. Catherine is very noble; she is perhaps an ideal human being. And yet, in the cosmos, she cannot be equated with the larger, diastolic reality; she cannot be placed at the same level.

Hence her death in the story is inevitable if we keep the Hemingway aesthetic in mind.

But her death does not cancel out the meaning of immediate life, or what she passed through and stood for in her life. Immediate life, while it lasts, is supreme; it will assert itself and offer areas of delight to the individual in innumerable ways. And the individual who is passive, who has put his will and ego to sleep, who is willing from time to time to subject himself to the diastolic periods of submission, will be more receptive to the immediacy of life than the one who comes to grips with it as a combatant or as a man of action. What Frederick and Catherine go through, separately and together, establishes this clearly.

4

The Short Stories

It is now accepted by almost every critic of Hemingway that the hero in his work deserves special attention. Philip Young sees the Hemingway protagonist as a sick man, wounded physically and psychically. Carlos Baker reads in him symbolic meanings, expressive of the contemporary emotional tensions. Leo Gurko has written a full-length book on the subject, for to him Hemingway's novels are essentially portrayals of the hero as the "individual man."[1] Thus, it is almost generally agreed that one of the important expressions of the Hemingway literary aesthetics is his hero. As it happens, his shorter fiction, now to be considered, offers as wide a scope as his novels for describing the Hemingway hero.

Most of Hemingway's stories were written between 1920 and 1940, a period of twenty years when Hemingway was making his name as a writer. Of the forty-nine stories published in the collected edition of 1938, some are very short, some very long; some are placed indoors, some outdoors; some are packed with action, some merely express a mood; some are told in the first person and some in the third; some narrate a single episode, some narrate a series of them, almost like a novel. In subject matter and the type of character portrayed they are varied too. The gallery of portraits includes farmers, doctors, priests, innkeepers, homosexuals, drug addicts, prostitutes, lesbians, hotel girls, hoodlums, thugs, fascists, burlesque managers, soldiers, jockeys, boxers, men of the waterfront, pirates, suicides, cooks, lumberjacks, barmen, waiters, and, of course, bullfighters.

It is a mistake to imagine that Hemingway wrote all these stories and sketches merely to promote or develop only one character—that is, Nick Adams. This is a miscalculation made by most critics of Hemingway; they have all tried to concentrate on Nick Adams. Superficially the stories give that impression, for you meet Nick in them at different age levels and his aging follows a chronological sequence. But artistically each story is complete in itself, a major aesthetic consideration when we try to see whether or not there is a link between the stories. The link between them is only the general association that always runs through the entire body of a writer's work; in no way is one story dependent on the other for the completion of its meaning. Thus, it would be more helpful to see each story separately and to think of Nick Adams in the plural rather than in the singular. There are many Nick Adamses in the stories, and the name does not necessarily identify the same character.

It would be more useful to imagine that Hemingway in these stories was concerned with a question of choice, of priorities. He seems to have put the stories, or the writing of them, to the same use as Shakespeare put his history plays; he thought out his ideas and his technique in them, and used them as a kind of workshop. If the Shakespearean hero—to continue the analogy—was initially worked out by Shakespeare in the Henry V trilogy, the Hemingway hero took shape for Hemingway in *In Our Time, Men Without Women,* and *Winner Take Nothing.* In the character of the young prince, Shakespeare moved away from the classical notion of hero to a hero whose greatness depended not on fate or acts of physical heroism but on his moral worth. Living in a corrupt world, Prince Henry is above the evil around him. In the great tragedies of Shakespeare, it was this aspect of the hero, his deep moral susceptibility, that was finally to emerge.

Hemingway, in his short stories, similarly toys with the idea of his hero. He had Nick Adams in mind from the beginning, for the simple reason that he knew this character rather intimately, based as it was on his own life. But he had as well several other types of humans before him. The preoccupation of the artist in these stories is therefore not so much with the development of a mythical figure based on one character as with the exploration and establishment of his preferences.

Philip Young, in *Ernest Hemingway*, seems to assume that each story was written to complete the development of Nick Adams, as if with each separate sketch something new were added on to Hemingway's presentation of that character. This is true insofar as physical details vary from story to story to accommodate the new age level at which Nick appears in them. But it does not appear that Hemingway consciously used a method of accretion in these tales. The conclusion Young reaches in his chapter on the Hemingway hero is: "He has seen a great deal of unpleasantness, not only in the war but . . . in Michigan as well; and he has been wounded by these experiences in a physical way, and—since the spine blow is both fact and symbol—also in a psychical way."[2] Beginning with the first story in *In Our Time*, and continuing through the stories in the order in which they appear in the book, he tells us each time: "This is Nick's initiation to pain" ("Indian Camp"); this teaches Nick "about the solidarity of the male sex" ("The Doctor and the Doctor's Wife");

this teaches about "a somewhat peculiar attitude toward women" ("The End of Something"), and so on. He adds confidently, "Nick is learning things,"[3] meaning thereby that the principal concern of Hemingway is Nick Adams and his complete identification with his hero.

But in the very next chapter of his book, Young offers the theory of what he calls the "code hero" in Hemingway. The code hero is what Hemingway's ideal concept of man is, his concept of honor and courage. To quote Young: "This code is very important because the 'code hero,' as he is . . . called, presents a solution to the problems of Nick Adams, of the true 'Hemingway hero,' and for Hemingway it was about the only solution."[4] This surely is confusing. Is Young for the code hero or the true hero, then? Who was Hemingway for?—for the code hero or the true hero? According to Young, Hemingway obviously was for the code hero, as the code gave Hemingway "about the only solution" he could think of for Nick Adams, his true hero. So who in the opinion of Young was the real Hemingway hero, the code hero or the true hero? If it was the code hero that really mattered to him, why should Hemingway have devoted all his stories to the development of a non-code hero, Nick Adams? And if the true hero, Nick Adams, is the real hero, what is the code hero doing here?

The simple explanation is that Hemingway in these stories is undertaking an enormous experiment. In addition to Nick, there are many characters in the stories who are substantially different individuals from Nick. To give a brief list, they are Doctor Adams, the He of "A Very Short Story"; Krebs of "Soldier's Home"; the I of "Now I Lay Me"; the I of "After the Storm"; the Old Waiter in "A Clean, Well-lighted Place"; the I of "The Light of the World"; Mr. Johnson and Mr. Harris in "Homage to

Switzerland"; Schatz of "A Day's Wait"; the I of "A Natural History of the Dead"; the I of "Wine of Wyoming"; the Mexican Gambler of "The Gambler, the Nun and the Radio"; Francis Macomber in "The Short Happy Life of Francis Macomber"; and Harry of "The Snows of Kilimanjaro". Then we have characters like Dick Boulton, or the Revolutionist, or My Old Man, or Manuel Garcia, Al and Max, Jack the Boxer, the Man of "The Sea Change," He of "The Mother of a Queen," Paco, and the big game hunter, Robert Wilson.

If we like, we may say that some of these characters are like Nick and that they supplement his image. But that would be oversimplifying the aesthetic issue involved. For Hemingway these characters are what they are; they represent no one but themselves. In the stories in which they appear, they are the center of attraction and Hemingway sees them as such. To give one example, the story "The Doctor and the Doctor's Wife," is about Doctor Adams, or perhaps it is about the doctor's wife or about the Indian, Dick Boulton, who picks the quarrel with the doctor. These are the main characters of the story, and none of them is identical with Nick.

Again, as far as plot goes, this story has nothing whatsoever to do with Nick, and it is difficult to see how Young reads the story as primarily about Nick. Nick has not watched the quarrel between his father and Dick Boulton, he has not heard the remarks of his mother addressed to his father; he is nowhere near the scene. And yet in Young's words, what has happened has revealed to Nick the companionship he can form with his father as a male and how unhappy and dissatisfied he is with his mother.[5] Later still, Young adds that Nick cannot bear his mother's inability to admit evil or come face to face with it.[6] One fails to understand how any of these observations is justifiable.

Hemingway's heroes are not "sick," nor are they particularly "heroic." The key word for understanding the Hemingway hero, according to my reading, is spontaneity. The Hemingway hero is a man immensely alive to everything, and in his spontaneity he has the vital capacity to react to life in innumerable and unpredictable ways.

That is the true Hemingway hero: a genuinely spontaneous individual. This kind of spontaneity is impossible to acquire unless one has learned the art of quieting the ego. Ultimately, therefore, the spontaneity gets tied up with creative passivity. The desire in his heroes is to feel everything *fully*—and therefore slowly, egolessly. "He did not want to rush his sensations any,"[7] says Hemingway about Nick in "Big, Two-Hearted River," and the expression is typical. The life of the trout, of the mink, and of the mosquitoes and the grasshoppers that is painted in the story comes rushing to Nick because of his extreme spontaneity, his extreme sensitivity to what is going on around him. In spite of what is commonly believed about his characters, Hemingway's heroes are not in the least egotistical. For egoism and sensitivity in an individual cannot go together. It is possible to have one or the other —not both. His hero thus acts from dark sources within his own self and is perennially in touch with the unknown of existence.

ii

We now go on to the structure of the stories. In the previous chapters it has been shown how Hemingway consummately brings the narration to a point of stillness and then introduces a pause in the story. The narrative at that time comes almost to a standstill. Both Carlos Baker and Philip Young, in their analyses of the stories, often point out how many of the stories seem to have no "point" to them, or how very often we do not know what the stories are about. Hemingway would have been too naïve an artist if he had pursued an art that was pointless or had nothing specific to achieve. Besides exploring varied human behavior in these stories, Hemingway is occupied here with an enormous structural innovation: the two-tier method of narration that was to impart such vitality to all his work. For clearly, in the stories we have the same pause in the narration, the same suspended movement, as that employed by Hemingway in his longer fiction. So structurally, as well as in his exploration of the nature of his hero, the stories were used by Hemingway as a workshop for experimentation.

As stated previously, in almost all the stories we can discover two distinct modes of action: systolic action and diastolic action. In the latter, which is the more important mode of the two, the systolic action comes to a standstill. These are moments when the entire systolic action that has preceded is in a way relived and consolidated, and the individual made ready for the next systolic move in the light of his experiences of the diastolic period. The moments of diastolic action are moments of return to one's deepest self; they are moments of mystical revelation. They are *not* moments of analysis, of self-analysis, or of "conscience," as Hemingway once cynically put it. These are moments when the individual recognizes, without the shadow of a doubt, that the rhythm of all life is much greater than that of his own individual self.

In the short stories, the diastolic action is introduced in two ways. Either the entire story is divided into two halves, not necessarily equal, where the first offers the systolic action and the second the diastolic. Or the diastolic action and the moments of pause are interspersed in the main movement of the story.

A few examples of the first kind are: "Indian Camp," "The Doctor and the Doctor's Wife," "The Battler," "Mr. and Mrs. Elliot," "Cross-Country Snow," "The Killers," "Ten Indians," "A Clean, Well-lighted Place," "One Reader Writes," and, in a special way, "The Undefeated," and "The Short Happy Life of Francis Macomber." The other kind, where the pauses are interspersed throughout the story, includes: "The End of Something," "Soldier's Home," "Cat in the Rain," "My Old Man," "Big Two-Hearted River," "Hills Like White Elephants," "Fifty Grand," "Now I Lay Me," "The Sea Change," "Fathers and Sons," and "The Snows of Kilimanjaro." Since the second kind requires greater craftsmanship, the stories where the diastolic action is interspersed are superior and structurally more complex.

iii

In the first type, where the story is neatly divided into two parts, one can almost draw a line across the page where the systolic action ends and the diastolic action begins. In "Indian Camp," up to the point where the Indian is found dead in the upper bunk with his throat cut, there is one particular movement of the story. Nick and his father, the doctor, are out in the shack where an Indian woman is having labor pains prior to the delivery of her child. Expertly the doctor takes control of the situation, expertly he explains to Nick what is happening, expertly he sets about the business of delivering the baby. Nick watches the entire scene, and from time to time his father enlarges on the various developments. The woman screams the whole while, and meanwhile her husband, unable to bear the tension, has cut his throat. His suicide is discovered right at the end of the systolic action. The doctor looks up in the bunk above and finds the man dead, with a pool of blood surrounding him. He makes an attempt to send Nick out of the shack but discovers that the boy has already seen the gory sight.

> There was no need of that. Nick, standing in the door of the kitchen, had a good view of the upper bunk when his father, the lamp in one hand, tipped the Indian's head back.[8]

Now, by every rule of construction, the story comes to an end here. It had a "plot" and that plot has been narrated. But a page of prose is still to follow, and that page does not concern itself directly with either the woman who has had the child or her dead husband. Nor does the page in any way analyze or dissect the action that has gone before.

What, then, is the significance of the last page, after we have drawn a line across the story, indicating an end of the systolic action? The page that follows is a perfect illustration of diastolic action or the pause. Nick and his father are alone now. They have been through an ordeal, in their own separate ways. And the experience has made them different, has transformed them somewhat—in spite of themselves.

There is no planning or motivation behind the conversation that ensues between the doctor and his son. Nick merely asks his father a few questions and his father replies.

"Do ladies always have such a hard time having babies?"
Nick asked.

"No, that was very, very exceptional."

"Why did he kill himself, Daddy?"

"I don't know, Nick. He couldn't stand things, I guess."

"Do many men kill themselves, Daddy?"

"Not very many, Nick."

"Do many women?"

"Hardly ever."

"Don't they ever?"

"Oh, yes. They do sometimes."

. . . . . .

. . . . . .

"Is dying hard, Daddy?"

"No, I think it's pretty easy, Nick. It all depends."[9]

The conversation shows that both the questions and the answers are inconsequential. What hits the reader is the unmistakable awareness of something larger than life that has just come to pass; their awareness of the dark mystery of life. Nick is only a boy, but the doctor is a seasoned practitioner, accustomed to the fact of death. But, in spite of his knowledge, even he is overpowered by what has happened. He tries to sound well-informed to his son, but his replies come haltingly, pensively. Even he realizes that there are mysteries that his ability and his mastery of factual knowledge cannot encompass. When Nick asks pointedly, "Why did he kill himself, Daddy?" the reply the doctor gives is: "I don't know, Nick. He couldn't stand things, I guess." The reply is an acceptance of the mystery which baffles man and ever remains beyond him.

Earlier in the story, in the systolic period, the same doctor is absolutely sure of himself. Explaining the biology of human birth to Nick, he confidently speaks of "muscles" and of "human screams" which come out when the muscles are trying to push the baby out and of the various "positions" in which the babies emerge from the womb. He knows, at that stage, what the demands of the moment are and finds himself competent to meet them expertly. But now, in the diastolic part, he is befuddled. He does not quite know if he knows all that there is to know about life—either in its beginnings or its denouement.

In the two sections of the story, the tone and the rhythm are different too. Straight narrative or ratiocinative analysis could not have achieved the deadly subtlety that the altered rhythm of the two sections offers. The reader is left almost speechless with pain, or the aesthetic consciousness of pain. Both Nick and his father have suffered and have to some extent aged in the story. The final impact is that of ripening or mellowing, and in the very last sentence, when Nick's hand is trailing in the water, while he and his father are rowing back to their home, and in the early morning chill, he suddenly feels "quite sure that he would never die." In this sentence forces of life and forces of death are brought to a curious, tangible clash and they seem to be equally powerful.

In "The Doctor and the Doctor's Wife," the line between the systolic action and the diastolic action is drawn at the point where Dick Boulton and his companions Eddy and Billy leave the doctor's yard after the row with him and the doctor returns to the bungalow. Again, the quarrel or the main episode that takes place in the systolic action is only a catalytic agent, not important in itself. It is important only because it sets off a reaction and forces self-discovery on some of the characters involved. In "Indian Camp" the persons to whom things actually happen in the systolic period are the

Indian woman and her husband. But neither these characters nor the incident in itself is of much value, standing alone or apart from the diastolic period that follows. The episode inside the shack is of importance only as it forces new mutations in Nick and his father.

Similarly in "The Doctor and the Doctor's Wife," in the first half, the systolic part of the story, the doctor has a row with Dick Boulton. Dick has come to saw some timber for the doctor. The logs have come down the lake. They have drifted away from the main raft, which was carrying them downstream to the mill. The doctor knows that sooner or later someone from the mill will come to collect these logs. But he assumes that some of them may be left to rot there for ever, and so he sends for Dick to come and cut up the logs for him to use as firewood. Dick brazenly tells the doctor that he is in fact stealing the logs. There is a heated exchange of words, after which Dick and his companions leave. The doctor has meantime gone back to the house in a huff.

This briefly is the systolic action of the story. Then follows the diastolic section, the section of creative passivity, when the shock that this dispute has given to the doctor compels a rediscovery in him. He suddenly realizes that what Dick had said had an odd kind of truth in it; he *was* in a way committing a theft. The sight of the unopened medical journals and the other mail, all symbolic of the life of activity and systolic action, depresses and irritates him. For surely he has now to live with the new awareness of himself, an awareness forced on him by a seemingly trivial incident. His wife drones along about the life of the "spirit," and he listens to her with indifference, his answers seldom amounting to more than monosyllables like "Yes" or "No."

He then takes out his gun and pensively cleans it. The

gun for him represents the life of the body, and its very touch is soothing to him. But he knows that even that is not the total truth of the matter. Neither the spiritual dogmas of his Christian Scientist wife nor the physical smoothness of life symbolized by the gun can contain him at this stage. When his wife asks him what the quarrel with Dick Boulton was about, the doctor replies, "Well, Dick owes me a lot of money for pulling his squaw through pneumonia and I guess he wanted a row so he wouldn't have to take it out in work," a reply which is no doubt substantially true. Maybe that is what Dick was after. But unintentionally he has hit the doctor hard somewhere in the inner recesses of his psyche, and unintentionally he has set off a chain reaction in the doctor which is more in the nature of a storm.

"Dear, I don't think, I really don't think that any one would really do a thing like that."

"No?" the doctor said.

"No. I can't really believe that any one would do a thing of that sort intentionally."

The doctor stood up and put the shotgun in the corner behind the dresser.

"Are you going out, dear?" his wife said.

"I think I'll go for a walk," the doctor said.[10]

In this exchange, the doctor is not quite being impatient with his wife. It is apparent that she is a woman with her mind made up about life and most of her expressions are only slogans or dogmas. But the doctor at the moment is not quite sure about it. If she has lived her life according to a formula, perhaps he has too. His formula happens to be a different one from hers; it is a formula all the same. The doctor goes out for a walk, and when he meets Nick in the garden and Nick wants to accompany him, he meditatively agrees. The story ends on a note of stillness, and leaves one with the unmistakable feeling of the complexity of the process of living, where no aspect in itself—neither the spirit, nor the body, nor the black squirrels in the trees—conveys the total meaning of existence. The total meaning is beyond man, it is too big, too shapeless. It contains good and evil, both. Most of all, it is so subtle that it defies verbalization.

It is essential to see that Hemingway's so-called pessimism is nowhere conceptually projected by Hemingway as such. What we have in his characters is a certain "acceptance"—an acceptance of the inevitable—and it is only by stretching the meaning of the word that we can think of this acceptance as pessimism. It is passivity, certainly, but it is creative passivity and is far removed from pessimism. For his characters come to realize that in the scheme of things their own contribution is but a limited one. And while the play of life lasts, their part in it is glorious. But eventually they must submit to something larger than themselves, something unnameable, unknowable, undefinable, but something very much there nevertheless.

The doctor in this story, and both Nick and his father in the story "Indian Camp," move from a systolic assertion of human knowledge and power to a diastolic acceptance of a power which includes man and yet is higher than man. "The Killers" further clarifies this. Why is it that Ole Andreson refuses to stir from the bed when Nick goes and tells him of the impending danger to his life? Why that inactivity? He is a champion fighter himself and not unfamiliar with personal peril. The sight of him, a strong man, stretched listlessly disconcerts Nick, and when he announces, "they said they were going to kill you," he immediately feels how silly he is in saying that to Ole Andreson.[11] For who would dare kill Ole Andreson, the great fighter? And yet, there is absolutely no response from Ole Andreson. He stays where he is. The story has now moved into the diastolic period, which begins at the time when Nick opens the door of the room where Ole Andreson is lying and walks in.

The question arises, why does Ole Andreson refuse to move from the bed and act? The answer is that he has intuitively realized that this is the end. He has had his days of glory, but the larger life of the universe, always bigger than he in any case, has today, in its own peculiar mutations, closed in on him. In his diastolic mood, he somehow senses death, which in Hemingway mythology is not an image of extinction but a contributory image of life. (See discussion of this below, where I consider "The Snows of Kilimanjaro.") The twin sister of life, death, is around him today, so why even try to do anything? The dialogue between Ole Andreson and Nick is spoken in utter stillness. Nick offers to go and inform the police for him, but Ole Andreson resolutely refuses: "No. . . . That wouldn't do any good." Nick asks if there is anything else that he might do, and again Ole Andreson says: "No. There ain't anything to do." Nick hopefully suggests that maybe the whole thing is a bluff. Ole Andreson says: "No. It ain't just a bluff." "Couldn't you fix it up some way?" asks Nick, and Ole Andreson again says, "No."[12] There is a touch of nobility in this acceptance, and in the acceptance of the other heroes of Hemingway, and to label it as pessimism is to deny the dignity of that acceptance. Ole Andreson knows that the end is near, and that is that. The creative passivity makes him aware of the futility of any further resistance or action, and with an almost tragic dignity he is willing to accept what is unavoidable.

Manuel Garcia in "The Undefeated," on the other hand, is pushed into determined reflex action while in a mood of passivity. He is a poor, a mediocre bullfighter; at least on the surface he is nothing more than that. Normally we would have no sympathy for him for his repeated failures in the ring. We have no direct knowledge of these failures; we are only told about them. Yet when we meet him in the ring, we notice a reckless determination in him. Garcia's situation makes a striking contrast to that of Ole Andreson. Ole Andreson has ever been successful, Garcia has ever been a failure. Hence their diastolic realization of their "end" strikes them differently: from Ole Andreson it evokes graceful surrender, from Garcia a one last determined fight. Garcia is being goaded by the bull, and he is losing as usual. But we see that he is in reality taking unusual risks, as if he were fighting with life itself. The very movements or the passes over which the crowd would have roared in applause if performed by their favorite bullfighter pass unnoticed by it when executed by Manuel; the *El Heraldo* critic dismisses them as "vulgar." But by the time the story ends with Manuel fatally wounded, the old buffoon too has risen to tragic proportions. He knows he is a small fellow and life has kicked him about too often. But now that this is his last appearance in the ring (he had been warned about it earlier), he would meet life still, would come to terms with it— would challenge it, fight it, hurl defiance at it. In this final defiance, coming out of the implicit acceptance by him of his own limitations, of his own littleness as a fighter, Manuel achieves glory and is indeed great. He dies, but like Francis Macomber, he dies happy—dies "undefeated."

We shall now consider "The Short Happy Life of Francis Macomber," which from the technical standpoint is a very special kind of story. Hemingway offers innumerable nuances of human response in it, and the principal subject of the story is what is the principal subject of his entire fiction—human selfhood. What is man? What is he made of? What is it that lends glory to him? What is it that makes a "man" of a man? Is it physical courage? Is it love? Is it passion? Is it the pursuit of an ideology? What then?

The reply Hemingway seems to come up with is that there is really no answer to these issues; no single answer. Heroism, love, passion, patriotism, dying for a cause or an ideology, are all attributes of the great man, but none of them alone will suffice or tell the whole truth. There are things which will still escape us, attributes of reality which man can only glimpse and not grasp. That is what brings about the pang or pain in his major characters, his true heroes. Sensitivity in Hemingway is another expression, along with spontaneity, of being aware of this pang or pain of living. When there is no pain, the hero functions at a very limited level as an individual. His major characters are men and women who are all the while aware of the insufficiency of life, of its essential incompleteness. They are men and women who are conscious of the seeming separation from some ideal life, some higher life which man lacks and can discover in a few given moments if he has the luck. The sleepless nights which Nick or some of the other characters in the short stories pass are not nights passed in personal fear. Neither do their reveries represent the musings of chronic insomniacs. Rather, they show the extent to which these characters are disturbed by the manifest largeness of life, its apparent magnitude and depth. In the process, these characters themselves, whether in the short stories or the novels, paradoxically end up by being larger than the average human being. For in their realization of the limitations of man, in their sharp sensitivity, lies their dignity and nobility. The compelling force in them which drives them past all bounds in their quest, at times even making them look ridiculous in their search, ultimately raises these characters to sublime heights.

"The Short Happy Life," in its systolic stance gives us an account of how Francis Macomber has behaved like a coward while lion hunting in Africa. The hunt is graphically described for us, particularly the scene where Macomber runs away when he sees the lion. Hence he is clearly a coward, at least for Robert Wilson and his black gunbearers. He is also a coward for his wife, Margaret Macomber, who at once proceeds to confirm this for us by kissing Wilson on the mouth the moment the two men return to the car after the lion is finally shot dead by Wilson.

But the problem is not so simple as that. Hemingway was certainly fascinated by men like Wilson, who represented for him the pinnacle of human vitality. On that level the story provided Hemingway the scope for developing the life of action and of the senses, and Hemingway concentrates much of his artistic talent (and seems to be enjoying doing it) on the delineation of Wilson. But it appears that the conflicts involved in the story are of a deeper kind, and pitching Macomber against Wilson in an either/or fashion does not reflect the full impact of the story. These conflicts concern rather the lion inside the human heart and the terrors locked up there; they concern the problem of human relationships. The story therefore is really about Macomber, and his wife, Margaret, with whom his basic clash lies. She represents the success-oriented American woman—"the hardest, the cruelest, the most predatory and the most attractive."[13] She was a beauty queen at one time, and married a man, also handsome and urbane like herself. But since there was no creative bond between them, they drifted apart and instead of being lovers they became enemies.

The external event in the story, the lion hunt, is employed skillfully by Hemingway to make us aware of this inner conflict. The event in itself is also of major significance—at least in the technique of its presentation, where the lion seems so real that it almost becomes a character in the story. But more important, it helps bring into the open what was previously submerged. These two, Macomber and Margaret, had lived their life at the physical plane only. With age, with the passing away of personal charms, the physical came to be an even more obsessive need for them—at least for the wife. And when Macomber runs away from the lion, she has the ready impetus to brand him as a coward and turn from him to another man.

The night before, when Macomber hears the lion roar, he is genuinely afraid—a perfectly natural reaction from a man who has never heard this sound before. But at the breakfast table next morning, his wife is concerned only with her excitement:

> "What's the matter, Francis?" his wife asked him.
> "Nothing," Macomber said.
> "Yes, there is," she said. "What are you upset about?"
> "Nothing," he said.
> "Tell me," she looked at him. "Don't you feel well?"
> "It's that damned roaring," he said. "It's been going on all night, you know."
> "Why didn't you wake me?" she said. "I'd love to have heard it."[14]

In the conversation that follows she keeps up that tone and one at once discerns her general insensitivity to Macomber and his fears. The lion is shot all right, but by Wilson and not by Macomber. So poor Macomber is branded as a coward. His wife leaves him in the middle of the night to go to bed with Wilson. He wakes up when she is away and learns of his shame. "You don't wait long when you have an advantage, do you?" says he to his wife, when she returns after her visit to Wilson:

"Please let's not talk. I'm so sleepy, darling."
"I'm going to talk."
"Don't mind me then, because I'm going to sleep." And she did.[15]

That particular point in the story marks the end of the systolic narration. Now begins the diastolic part, which is not a movement forward in the horizontal direction. The events of the day, the bungling with the lion, and the open desertion by his wife have brought to bear on Macomber a totally unexpected and unanticipated pressure. What happens next is a kind of explosion. Not a violent explosion; no quarrels or blame-throwing; no bickering. That would be continuing the story on the same horizontal plane of narration. The unknown has somehow come and taken possession of Macomber now. The shock is too much, and the revelation equally too much—completely beyond his control. In the past he had tried to hang on to Margaret, even when he knew that their marriage was not based on creative unity. Now he suddenly sees Margaret as an inconsequential agent in the scheme of things—or at least not so consequential as he had imagined her to be. Perhaps Margaret will have to go now. Perhaps they will separate. Perhaps he will miss lions in the future as well. None of that really matters to him at the moment. What takes hold of him now is a duty to himself, a duty to his own inner self, which he had in the past ignored or not faced squarely. In the past he had not necessarily lived as a coward, but as a man in fear—in fear of Margaret, in fear of himself. That fear now vanishes from his thinking. There is a deeper reality that he has to search, a deeper debt that he owes. That reality is himself; that debt is to his own inner being. It is this awareness that brings about the transformation in him and he ceases to be afraid.

The story thereby is clearly divided into two parts. From here on till the end, we meet a different Macomber. But the action of the second half of the story is not to be seen as systolic action. It is rather a presentation of the diastolic reflex of Macomber. The new awareness that Macomber has cannot be translated into words, for Macomber does not quite know what this awareness is. It is still at the unspoken or unverbalized level. Hence Hemingway paints this awareness for us through reflex action, one representation of which is the dramatic sequence when Macomber ignores everyone and regardless of personal safety keeps firing at the bull when the bull comes charging at him. Both Wilson and Margaret are shocked at the new Macomber they see. Margaret herself finds the new awareness in Macomber too much for her. She can sense that it is something big and unnameable and maybe Macomber will be too much of a man for her now. ("He *would* have left you too,"[16] Wilson says to her.) In an instant she shoots and kills him. It all happens in an instant. But it would be wrong to describe the activity of Macomber here as systolic action. It is the diastolic touch that, as in the case of Manuel Garcia and Ole Andreson, prompts him to graceful self-assertion or self-extinction.

Thus "The Short Happy Life" too is an illustration of the two types of action in Hemingway—the systolic action and the diastolic action. What happens at the diastolic level is the more important, for it is at that level, when the main movement of the story is brought to a stillness, that revelations take place, that new selves are discovered, and that life acquires a meaning which includes the physical but transcends it and goes far beyond it.

iv

Let us now consider the stories in which the pause is interspersed throughout the story. There is action and then inactivity; action again, again inactivity. And perhaps we should begin with "Big Two-Hearted River," which is a great story and typical of Hemingway's technique.

Philip Young considers "Big Two-Hearted River" the story of a "sick man," who at the same time is running away from "whatever it is that made him sick."[17] This is not a new conclusion for Young; for him every story or novel of Hemingway presents a picture of a sick man. But the reasoning by which he arrives at this conclusion is not very clear.

Nick Adams is decidedly not a sick man in this story, for the one simple reason that his preoccupations and concerns throughout are with living things. The neurotic is almost dead to the world around him. He is so morbidly taken up with his own ego that his sensitivity to life or his sensitivity to others is reduced to a minimum. Nothing matters to him but his own small self, blown out of all proportions. He alone is the center of the universe; he the most important entity.

Does Nick give us that impression in the story? On the contrary, we notice that the story pulsates with a multiplicity of life, human as well as nonhuman, and that Nick is acutely aware of this. Nick is not seen in isolation from that nonhuman life, nor is he contrasted to it. He is seen as a part of that bigger life, which includes him but also includes a variety of other life. That is how Hemingway plans the story and that seems to be the intention behind it: to speak of the river of life which is "big," so big that it is "two-hearted."

Failing to see that, we fail to see the magnitude of the tale. The moment Nick gets off the train and walks into the territory of the river, it is the larger life of the universe spread around him that comes and confronts him. The trout are drifting along the current or they are jumping out of the river into the shadow of the sun; a kingfisher is flying up the stream; the dark pines rise in solitary grandeur; a host of grasshoppers, "sooty black" in color, dart out of the dust and one of them starts nibbling at Nick's woolen socks; sweet fern grows ankle high along the path and millions of insects fly along the line of the river. And throughout the story, while Nick is fishing, he remains conscious of the beauty of this universe, a universe that is self-evolving and independent of man and man's ingenuity, and that in its glory far surpasses the glories of man.

Malcolm Cowley has referred to the story as something of a "walking dream" on the part of Nick. He says, it is an escape for Nick either from a nightmare or "from realities that have become a nightmare."[18] Again, it is difficult to appreciate the comment. Where is any indication of nightmare in the story? Nick does have occasional nostalgic feelings about the past, when he sees his old haunt, the river, once again. But surely we are not going to confuse nostalgia with nightmare?

The story has to be considered as an example of the sensitive, deeply "aware" hero of Hemingway fiction that we have elsewhere. Nick Adams is a man alive to the world around him, open to it and conscious of its glory. The entire story is told in a most relaxed mood rather than one of hurry and tension. Philip Young finds the movement of the story "monotonous," "unrelieved by even a phrase of comment or a break in the rhythm." This he says about Part I of the story. Speaking of Part II, he repeats his observations concerning "chronologically ordered, mechanical, deliberate movements which begin to wear on one's nervous system."[19] To me, the movement suggests a completely different intent and results.

In *Green Hills of Africa* the narrator (presumably Hemingway himself) and his wife and a few friends are talking about the arts, especially the art of writing. And the narrator speaks of the ultimate kind of writing, which has never been attempted but which can be done:

> "What is this now?"
>
> "The kind of writing that can be done. How far prose can be carried if anyone is serious enough and has luck. There is a fourth and fifth dimension that can be gotten."
>
> "You believe it?"
>
> "I know it."
>
> "And if a writer can get this?"
>
> "Then nothing else matters. It is more important than anything he can do. The chances are, of course, that he will fail. But there is a chance that he succeeds."
>
> "But that is poetry you are talking about."
>
> "No. It is much more difficult than poetry. It is a prose that has never been written. But it can be written, without tricks and without cheating. With nothing that will go bad afterwards."[20]

This is an extraordinary and somewhat rare defense of the art of writing that Hemingway himself was doing. But it is an even more extraordinary defense of prose as a medium of communication in preference to poetry. Fielding once said that if Homer had written his epics in prose, they would have been even greater books than they are now. Hemingway shows a similar faith in the power of prose.

Malcolm Cowley dismisses the "fifth dimension" as a "mystical or meaningless figure of speech,"[21] but it is a new kind of prose that Hemingway is speaking of here, and though in the next paragraph he enumerates several qualities that might produce this prose, he does not explain the aesthetic nature of the prose itself. He speaks of "talent," of "discipline," of "conception," of "absolute conscience," of "intelligence," of "disinterestedness," but that does not include everything. "Try to get all these in one person and have him come through all the influences that press on a writer," he says. And then he says: "The hardest thing, because time is so short, is for him to survive and get his work done." Now, the last sentence may be taken as an indication of the proverbial pessimism of Hemingway, but that is not necessarily so. The last sentence is in a way very vital. Hemingway is always conscious of the "indescribable" element in life. There is always something that escapes man. Unless that were so, man would be perfect and complete in himself. Something is invariably left out, whether the search is for the ultimate truths or the human self.

Likewise, in good prose there is a factor that remains beyond the level of conscious formulation. But with luck a writer can get there, or get very close to it. That is the fourth and fifth dimension of existence, which somehow one reaches—by a leap, as it were.

In "Big Two-Hearted River," Hemingway reaches that perfection of prose, for the story is a tale of pure sensuous pulsation of the universe. It is that extremely delicate awareness which accepts life with its secret cognitions on faith—it is *that* which comes and takes control of Nick when he goes on the fishing expedition in his native Michigan.

The story opens with the arrival of Nick in the old countryside, where he notices that meanwhile the land has been burned out. Now the systolic and the diastolic states alternate from the beginning and they come and go all the time. There is the physical countryside around Nick and his fishing in it that represent the systolic action. And then there is what the country does to him. That is the diastolic action.

"Nick's heart tightened as the trout moved. He felt all the old feeling."[22] We are in the diastolic state with this sentence. He sees the trout, the trees, and of course the river stretched out before him, and he stops in his tracks. The forward, horizontal connections of the story are broken. Our motion in time is halted. It is unwarranted to conclude from this that Nick is sick or is trying to find an escape from a nightmare. What comes over him when he sees the familiar countryside is a feeling of gladness, which is different from the feeling of compulsive relief that mental illness or nightmare compels one to seek. "He was happy," Hemingway tells us plainly enough.

> From the time he had gotten down off the train and the baggage man had thrown his pack out of the open car door things had been different. Seney was burned, the country was burned over and changed, but it did not matter. It could not all be burned. He knew that.[23]

Happy with himself, Nick starts walking, trying to find a camping place, and apparently the story is moving at the systolic level again. But he stops for a smoke and we are back in the diastolic stage.

> Carefully he reached his hand down and took hold of the hopper by the wings. He turned him up, all his legs walk-

ing in the air, and looked at his jointed belly. Yes, it was black too, iridescent where the back and the head were dusty.

"Go on hopper," Nick said, speaking out loud for the first time. "Fly away somewhere."[24]

Another walk, and another period of rest follow, this time in the sweet fern: another systolic period, and another diastolic.

He lay on his back and looked up into the pine trees. His neck and back and the small of his back rested as he stretched. The earth felt good against his back. He looked up at the sky, through the branches, and then shut his eyes. He opened them and looked up again. There was a wind high up in the branches. He shut his eyes again and went to sleep.[25]

The peace of the passage is self-evident. Young finds the rhythm of the story unvaried. But the passages cited above, referring to the diastolic stance, are distinct and apart from the passages where Nick is actually doing something. There the story moves faster. Nick is busy in action: catching grasshoppers, or pulling the trout in, or pitching the tent, or opening a can of beans. But the cadence of the other passages is slower, as may be seen above. "The earth felt good against his back." It is the feeling of mother earth or mother nature posed here—a feeling of the "beyond," which can only be briefly touched.

Then we are familiarized in the story with many local smells, all of which Nick finds "good." "His hands smelled good from the sweet fern";[26] "It smelled pleasantly of canvas"[27]; "There was a good smell."[28] In Part II, we read of Nick's camp as a "good" camp. Is that atmosphere, or Nick's reaction symptomatic of the paranoid? Nick has simply come to revisit his "old man" river. He was not less happy than most other men, from what we read in the story. He had not come here looking for a refuge, or an escape. It is just a visit. But as soon as he gets here, the greater life of the countryside overwhelms him, and he becomes aware of the greater mystery of life, the greater holiness of it.

An important passage in the story is when Nick, having pitched his tent, crawls into it:

> Inside the tent the light came through the brown canvas. It smelled pleasantly of canvas. Already there was something mysterious and homelike. Nick was happy as he crawled inside the tent. He had not been unhappy all day. This was different though. Now things were done. There had been this to do. Now it was done. It had been a hard trip. He was very tired. That was done. He had made his camp. He was settled. Nothing could touch him. It was a good place to camp. He was there, in the good place. He was in his home where he had made it. Now he was hungry.[29]

The passive, the creatively passive, surrender of the individual to the cosmos is extremely well conveyed. Nick has now reestablished his contact with the unknown. It is very much like the Zen concept of an individual's relatedness to the life around him. The life of the individual has a meaning only in the corporate life of the total universe.

The actual fishing is done in Part II of "Big Two-Hearted River." With meticulous care, and with much delight, Hemingway gives us every single detail of the machinery and mechanism of fishing: from the point where the bait is prepared to the pulling in of the trout, we are told that Nick is "excited" or "happy" or is having

a "good feeling." The pulse of the cosmos beats mysteri-
ously around him and he is an integral part of that cosmos.
The systolic and diastolic pattern is also maintained in
Part II. Frequently the forward movement of the story
comes to a halt, and we see Nick reveling in his present
sensation: "He did not want to rush his sensations any."
At the moment, the sensation is one of disappointment
because he has just lost a good trout. But notice the
quiescence, the tranquillity:

> He wriggled his toes in the water, in his shoes, and got
> out a cigarette from his breast pocket. He lit it and tossed
> the match into the fast water below the logs. A tiny trout
> rose at the match, as it swung around in the fast current.
> Nick laughed. He would finish the cigarette.
> He sat on the logs, smoking, drying in the sun, the sun
> warm on his back, the river shallow ahead entering the
> woods, curving into the woods, shallows, light glittering,
> big water-smooth rocks, cedars along the bank and white
> birches, the logs warm in the sun, smooth to sit on, without
> bark, gray to the touch; slowly the feeling of disappoint-
> ment left him.[30]

And so the story goes on, then finally closes with the
promise of many more happy days for Nick. For the river
of life is truly "big" and "two-hearted," and it has spells
enough to hold him for a lifetime.

In many other stories, Hemingway again tried the
interspersed method of spacing out the two movements
of narration. The ultimate purpose in all of them is to
make us conscious of the larger life of the universe, seen
through what happens to the protagonists. In "The End
of Something," is the negative awareness of the end of an
emotion, though Nick does not quite know what it is or
how to say it to Marjorie. In "Soldier's Home," it is Krebs'

metamorphosis that we see. His statement to his mother, "I don't love anybody," comes after that metamorphosis or self-realization has taken place in him. He has been away from home and he has seen war and men suffering and dying. His return to a world of "defined alliances and shifting feuds" does not make sense after what he has been through. And back home, he suddenly sees that the entire business of living means striking some kind of a pose, a farce. So he is no longer interested in anything— in politics, or in courting; not because he wants to cut himself off from life but because he does not want to strike any more poses—"He did not want to tell any more lies."[31] So, as a matter of fact, in this withdrawal he takes himself closer to the actual rhythm of life, which is spontaneous, free, and vital, and is devoid of farces.

One notices similar self-discoveries in "Cat in the Rain," "My Old Man," "Hills Like White Elephants," "Fifty Grand," "Now I Lay Me," "The Sea Change," "Fathers and Sons," and in "The Snows of Kilimanjaro." After the experience of the story, the protagonist is changed or transformed in some way for good.

The last story, "The Snows of Kilimanjaro," deserves special mention. The story was first published in 1936. By then Hemingway was moving slowly to the realization that the larger life of the universe must include an intuitive awareness of the mystery of Death; as early as 1932, in *Death in the Afternoon* he had commented on it. For the cosmic order of the universe could be maintained only through as powerful a balancing force on the other side as life on this one. Here Hemingway goes very close to the Christian mysticism of Boehme, where duality is seen at the center of everything. In the latter half of his creative career, Hemingway concerned himself with death in an increasingly intense fashion. *Across the River and*

Into the Trees and *The Old Man and the Sea* are fine studies of death and are powerful, creative reconstructions of the force of death. But in "The Snows of Kilimanjaro" we have a good foretaste of this.

The systolic-diastolic rhythm is most consummately presented in "The Snows," so much so that, by giving some of the passages in the story in a different type face, in italics, Hemingway himself seems to be subscribing to the theory. There is hardly any physical action in the story, as our hero is confined to bed with gangrene and cannot move. His mind is wandering and there are series of flashbacks, through which we see his earlier life and his relationships. But slowly in the story even the minimal systolic action is further reduced and then totally abandoned. By the time the story is over, diastolic action has taken over completely. And so has death taken over from life. And in a way the story becomes, in the series of clashes between the systolic and the diastolic actions, a struggle between life and death.

But the italicized passages are not to be seen as flashbacks, strictly speaking. For flashbacks imply a psychological departure into the past, which is not the aesthetic design followed by Hemingway in his fiction. For Harry, the hero of the story, these are very real moments, indicative of the present tense rather than the past. The passages are italicized by the author to give the reader the feel of an altered rhythm. The subject of these passages is not a vicarious longing for the past, but something very much alive to Harry. The subject is death.

On the surface it looks as though Harry in these passages is thinking of his early life. Memories of the war, his earlier love affairs, his fishing and hunting trips of the past, his days in Paris, do come and crowd his mind at the moment. But these images he recalls not to find refuge or support for his present fate.

These passages are representative of Harry's departure into another type of consciousness, and the memories are rather a symbolic projection of his current awareness. Right from the beginning of the story, we see Harry's intuitive feeling that he is going to die. While traveling through the African bush in Tanganyika, a writer has hurt himself. A thorn scratched his flesh and the wound became septic and now gangrene has set in too. The man knows that this is the end. "I'm dying now," he tells his wife and the vultures gathered round him seem to support his fears.

But these fears of his are thus far at the systolic level. Thus far he is thinking of death merely as an event in time. Like every other human, he is afraid of it; like everyone else he wants to avoid it and save his life. And since he knows he cannot, since he knows that gangrene is usually fatal, he is bitter with himself and his wife— more than usually bitter.

A very remarkable thing now happens in the story. But before we take note of it, it is worthwhile to consider the epigraph with which the story begins and which has been interpreted variously by Hemingway scholars. The epigraph gives a composite image of a snow-covered mountain peak, a peak called "the House of God," and "the dried and frozen carcass" of a leopard. It is essential not to split up the image into two units, as some critics have done ("fundamental moral idealism" versus "aimless materialism," or "integrity" versus "carelessness"). The snow-covered mountain and the carcass of the leopard represent a single image having a plural significance. The single composite image that the epigraph presents is that of Life-and-Death, *not* taken separately but *together*. Life is beautiful and great. But death walks hand in hand with it.

The remarkable development that takes place in the story is that Harry, instead of considering death as an event in time as he had to begin with and perhaps has done all his life, comes to look upon it as a living presence. The story thereafter unfolds the slow arrival of death at his side—its physical arrival. With the onset of gangrene the physical pain has stopped, and he no longer has that pressure on his nervous system to keep him in fear of the event. "Since the gangrene started in his right leg he had no pain and with the pain the horror had gone and all he felt now was a great tiredness and anger that this was the end of it." We read: "For years it had obsessed him; but now it meant nothing in itself."[32]

So the fear of the event has actually stopped, at least for the time being. But at the other level, the diastolic level, another kind of awareness is coming into existence. It is slow in appearing, but once the process has started it gathers momentum. His death is now not an event for him in time, but a weird companion of life, and just as at one time life had possessed the soul of Harry completely, now death was going to take possession of him as completely.

This realization is made final for him through a clever factual insertion by Hemingway in the plot of the story, and by his tying up this factual bit with the awareness of death in Harry's consciousness. Harry is a professional writer, and it is not the loves of his life, or his quarrels, for that matter (the last of them, with his present wife Helen, still with him), or his days in Paris, or his fishing and hunting expeditions, or his adventures in the war—it is none of these things that at heart he cares about. What he really cares about is his writing, his ability to transmit or communicate experience through words. He sees clearly that with death around he would never be able to communicate life any longer. He is thus in a state of ulti-mate knowledge, when he knows that he is entering a new region that has its own terms of reference. Death is not an event that will just cut him off from life; death is a territory imposing its own aesthetic requirements.

Those are requirements of an unfamiliar order and Harry realizes that "now he would never write the things that he had saved to write."[33] At the systolic level, this realization emerges in the form of self-accusations: "He had destroyed his talent by not using it, by betrayals of himself and what he believed in, by drinking so much that he blunted the edge of his perceptions, by laziness, by sloth, and by snobbery, by pride and by prejudice, by hook and by crook."[34] But at the diastolic level he has no doubt about his ability; he is conscious of things that he still might have done had he been spared. His talent has not altogether vanished or been destroyed. Only a bigger thing has now come along, this death, and it wants to take him along with it.

None of the five italicized passages in the story represents "memories," but subjects on which Harry could still write. These passages by implication show his realization of death. They—those subjects—are remembered by him in the context of the impending end, which is going to remove him from them. The diastolic reality subjects him to a wider vision, in which he sees the vaster potentialities which remained unfulfilled. "But he had never written a line of that," is his response—not a line. While at the systolic level he blames himself for the delay; at the diastolic level he accepts the delay as perhaps inevitable, as a period of preparation—for all the time he knew that he "would write it finally."

There was so much to write. He had seen the world change; not just the events; although he had seen many of them and had watched the people, but he had seen the subtler change and he could remember how the people were at different times. He had been in it and he had watched it and it was his duty to write of it; but now he never would.[35]

"But now he never would." The phrase strikes one as not a statement of regret so much as of a weird realization of the approach of that other master force, the master companion of life—death.

As the story proceeds, Harry's awareness of death becomes sharper. His wife has just returned with some game for him which she has shot, and in the evening they are having a drink together. Harry is feeling remorseful for having been so bitter to her in the morning. He thinks she *is* a good woman, considerate all the time—"marvellous really." And then, for the first time in the story, his diastolic realization of death comes on him. He is in fact at the moment talking of other things, his mind not preoccupied with dying. But all at once he senses death:

> It came with a rush; not as a rush of water nor of wind; but of a sudden evil-smelling emptiness and the odd thing was that the hyena slipped lightly along the edge of it.[36]

The parallel images of the "rush of water" or the "rush of wind," and their rejection as suitable similes is purposeful. For with this rejection Hemingway is trying to establish the "otherness" of death. Even "evil-smelling emptiness" is not enough, so that another image, that of the hyena slipping "lightly along the edge of it," has to be brought in to establish the reality which cannot be communicated through words or language. But that Harry does sense a presence near him and is startled by it, we are left in no doubt. His wife notices this, and asks: "What is it, Harry?" And he answers: "Nothing . . . You had better move over to the other side. To windward."[37]

But from now on, he cannot seem to get rid of the sense

of death. His wife goes away to have her bath and when she returns and they are about to eat, he senses it once again. "This time there was no rush. It was a puff, as of a wind that makes a candle flicker and the flame go tall."[38] The whole thing is done very inventively, bordering on the occult. Harry realizes that there is going to be a meeting, a strange meeting. "So this was how you died," he tells himself, "in whispers that you did not hear." But lying as he is in the diastolic peace, there is no fear of the unexpected. There is even a joy, an expectancy. After all, death is copartner of life, and this copartner was now going to manifest itself to him.

In none of his reactions in the diastolic period do we notice any misgivings in Harry: "The one experience that he had never had he was not going to spoil now." This establishes the utter strangeness of what is happening—a welcome strangeness. So he promises himself that he will do nothing to spoil the new feelings that were coming. He also tells himself: "He probably would. You spoiled everything. But perhaps he wouldn't."[39]

But an even more monumental transformation comes to pass at this stage. For years, as he has been reprimanding himself, Harry had written nothing. For years he had frittered away his creativity. But with the near arrival of death, with the arrival of something so new and so powerful, what happens is that his creativity also returns to him. He suddenly wants to write—this minute—now.

"You can't take dictation, can you?"
"I never learned," she told him.
"That's all right."
There wasn't time, of course, although it seemed as though it telescoped so that you might put it all into one paragraph if you could get it right.[40]

The systolic mood returns, and he again wants to hang on to life; he is by turns afraid of death and also attracted to it. "He lay still and death was not there. It must have gone around another street. It went in pairs, on bicycles, and moved absolutely silently on the pavements."[41] His wife nags him about his drinking but, unconcerned, he lapses into the diastolic mode and his mind roams over some of the stories that he could have written but never did. Once again he returns to the systolic mood and once again he does not wish to die. "He would rather be in better company."[42]

We are now very near the end of the story, and diastolic action almost completely takes over from the systolic. Death finally is back with him and the hour of the meeting has come. "Do you feel anything strange?" he asks his wife.

"No. Just a little sleepy."
"I do," he said.
He had just felt death come by again.[43]

The movement now resembles a nocturnal dance. Death keeps advancing at him and the scene of his surrender to that great power is vivid and powerful. He keeps talking to his wife, but his intuition is sharp. "What is that?" he asks himself,

Because, just then, death had come and rested its head on the foot of the cot and he could smell its breath.[44]

The moods come and go in flashes, and he tries to explain death to Helen. He is consciously aware by now that death has not one image but many, and none of the metaphors that he might employ would quite communicate what he is experiencing. It is like Wallace Stevens's

"Thirteen Ways of Looking at a Blackbird." Death is not merely "a scythe and a skull"; it could as easily be "two bicycle policemen," or "a bird," or the "wide snout" of a hyena. But he knows that it has many shapes, or rather no formal shape at all, which is another way of saying the same thing. "It had moved up on him now, but it had no shape any more. It simply occupied space."[45]

In the ultimate meeting with death, the systolic and the diastolic moods mingle intimately. At the systolic level, Harry wants to fight death. At the diastolic level he knows, it will offer him peace as nothing else ever had or ever could.

First comes the systolic fight. He tells his wife aloud to ask this thing to go away. But it "moved a little closer." And he can smell it now and he shouts: "You stinking bastard."

> It moved up closer to him still and now he could not speak to it, and when it saw he could not speak it came a little closer, and now he tried to send it away without speaking, but it moved in on him so its weight was all upon his chest, and while it crouched there and he could not move, or speak, he heard the woman say, "Bwana is asleep now. Take the cot up very gently and carry it into the tent."[46]

The fight, however, is soon over. But this story, or this kind of Hemingway story, must be distinguished from the story in which there is a clear division between the two movements. In the stories considered in the previous section, once we enter the diastolic mood, we stay there. Here the two movements alternate.

Harry is still not quite dead, but he has given himself over now to death in acceptance—in diastolic acceptance. In the long passage where the arrival of Compton and the subsequent departure of Harry by plane are narrated, Harry is still alive. It is Harry's consciousness which is conjuring up these pleasant images. And it is Hemingway's method of making us aware of the newness of the experience. No didactic passage in praise of death or its glory is ever introduced by Hemingway. The purity of the moment is never presented rhetorically. It comes to us in the form of narrative, and has to be known at the aesthetic level alone. But we see that Harry finds death a uniquely new experience from the fact that he is at least at peace with himself. While flying high in his imaginative vision, he looks down and sees "a new water that he had never known of." The plane then passes through a black waterfall, which is only rain falling very thickly. Once out of the rain, Compton turns his head toward Harry and points out to him their destination in the distance. And what does Harry see there? The square top of Kilimanjaro, "as wide as all the world, great, high, and unbelievably white in the sun."[47] Compie here is death who is taking Harry to the mountain of life. Harry dies with this knowledge, and the epigraph of the story becomes his epitaph.

v

The Hemingway hero that emerges in these stories is a highly sensitive individual, who derives his sensitivity from his ability to be in tune with the spirit of the universe. He is a highly passive human, by choice, as this enables him to respond to the cosmic rhythm more effectively. He values moments of action, but moments of creative resignation he values even more. He is not a particularly serene individual, but then, cultivated serenity is as much a pose as deliberate self-assertion, and he wants to be free of poses. He, however, has the capacity of true religious awareness of life. This awareness keeps him disturbed most of the time—that restlessness or disturbance being a part of the very design of living—but now and then he lapses into an unusual calm. The calm is not of his own making; it comes to him from the outside. At such moments he is more like a mystic than a man of action.

5

For Whom the Bell Tolls

i

After the conclusion of the last chapters, it may be ironical to be dealing with a hero, and with a novel, where physical action does seem to be the main concern of the novelist. The entire story of *For Whom the Bell Tolls* revolves around a physical feature, the blowing up of the bridge. Robert Jordan is most of the time "doing" things. There is no withdrawal of the individual into himself; rather such moments are determinedly pushed aside by the hero for the job in hand.

In the structure, too, the novel does not seem to distinguish itself very well. The story is told from the omniscient point of view. The all-seeing eye of the novelist jumps from place to place, from person to person, and now he is describing Robert Jordan on the hill and now El Sordo many miles away and now André Marty even further away. He works through as many varied consciousnesses —a single scene, like an evening in the cave, at times is described through the consciousness of Robert Jordan, then through that of Pilar, and yet again through the consciousness of Pablo.

Also, there are far too many characters in the story, and Hemingway wastes too much time in developing some of them when they are not necessary to the plot. The entire account of El Sordo seems too long-winded and unwarranted; so does the lengthy characterization of characters like Agustín or Fernando or Gomez or Lt. Berrendo.

As far as Hemingway's view of life is concerned, *For Whom the Bell Tolls* gets nowhere near the complexity of *The Sun Also Rises* or what was later to come in *The Old Man and the Sea*.

How then explain this novel within the framework of the Hemingway aesthetics that we have developed?

ii

To understand the value of *For Whom the Bell Tolls*, it is necessary to know the conditions in which the novel was produced. The thirties were a period when almost every writer, novelist or poet, was compelled to reexamine his obligation to the society in which he functioned. Political and historical events, in Europe and in the United States, shook the complacency of even those artists who had not been upset by the world war. There was a new star on the horizon, the star of Communism, which spoke of bread instead of beauty. In the United States, Communism was a distant force, but the Depression produced very nearly the same situation and a similar response.

All this time, Hemingway had resolutely refused to be involved with the political movements of the day. As Carlos Baker narrates in *Ernest Hemingway, A Life Story,* not even his "persuaders," who criticized him for his non-involvement, could make him change his stand.[1] With the outbreak of the Spanish Civil War, however, Hemingway's innate taste for the dramatic made him accept a position with the North American Newspaper Alliance and he went over to Spain to report the war. Till then he had showed no active partisanship for any of the social or political movements, at home or abroad. Even the trip to Spain must be seen more in the light of adventure than political alignment; that Martha Gellhorn, Hemingway's new sweetheart, was also going there as a journalist may have been an additional reason for the trip. But there was no political concern in the move. He was a writer; his main business was to keep himself alive and do his job. He did not alter his stand from the position he had maintained for so many years.

But something happened to Hemingway, while he was out there reporting the civil war. It is customary to link *To Have and Have Not, The Fifth Column,* and *For Whom the Bell Tolls,* as though they were the works of a similar influence or state of mind. But *To Have and Have Not* was already completed before Hemingway left for Spain in 1937 (he continued the revision of the manuscript, however, while he was in Spain). Moreover, the novel does not deal with a political system or a set of political values. It deals with the evils of revolution, true. But the characters involved do not care one bit for the revolution or for one system in preference to the others.

The two works produced directly after the impact of the Spanish war were *The Fifth Column* and *For Whom the Bell Tolls. The Fifth Column* was completed by November, 1937, on Hemingway's second visit to the Spanish war-torn soil. Hemingway was already perceptibly changed by then. In the world war, the men had fought for a dying cause, the dying order of the old imperialist Europe. No wonder the young men of the day came out of the war as a "lost generation." But the Spanish war was different. It was a war in favor of a growing ideology, a new cause. And Hemingway, in spite of his self-imposed withdrawal from socio-political entanglements, could not help being caught in the fever of the day.

The title of the article he wrote in March, 1938, for the newly founded leftist magazine *Ken* was typical of the current mood of Hemingway; it said, "The Time Now, The Place Spain." That he should agree to associate himself openly with a leftist magazine—he was announced as one of its editors—is itself indicative of the change. A few months before, when he was back in New York after his first trip to Spain, he even attended a promotional dinner in behalf of the same magazine, and sat conspicuously on the left of David Smart, the publisher.[2] Hemingway later often insisted that the Spanish war had been for him the turning point in his career.

Hemingway may have been in these pronouncements somewhat theatrical (as he often was). Nor did he maintain the same sense of personal association with the political atmosphere of the day for long. But at least for the period when *The Fifth Column* and *For Whom the Bell Tolls* were written, he felt genuinely indignant at the social injustice in the world. When *The Fifth Column* was being adapted for stage production in 1938, Hemingway insisted that the new version should not show the Communist party or the Spanish Republic in an adverse light.[3] And when *For Whom the Bell Tolls* was completed, Hemingway's own assessment of the novel was that it attempted three things: a credible love story, a unified action sequence, and the willingness of men and women to die for a cause.[4] In the make-up of a Hemingway novel, the last was surely a new factor.

For Whom the Bell Tolls thereby is a novel not so much about "action" as about "ideology." The epigraph from Donne, beginning "no man is an Iland, intire of it selfe," was borrowed by Hemingway only after the novel was completed; he did not project the story with this extreme sense of brotherhood in mind. But he did project it as the involvement of a few characters with an ideology and the obligations which any ideology imposes on the individual.

It should be observed, however, that, in spite of the fact that Robert Jordan is most of the time "doing" things in the novel, he is by nature a passive individual. Left to himself, he would rather be a writer, as he so often says in the novel, or make love, or breed horses; he is a revolutionary only by necessity. The only difference between Frederick Henry and Robert Jordan is that in the case of the new hero, he happens to believe in the ideology under which he is living. Frederick Henry somehow could not accept that it was "his" war. Robert Jordan on the other hand is convinced of the righteousness of the cause of the Republic. But that does not show that he is an active advocate of that cause. He insists that it is not his business to plan things out or to promote causes. "That was Golz's business. He had only one thing to do and that was what he should think about and he must think it out clearly and take everything as it came along, and not worry."[5]

It is true that *For Whom the Bell Tolls* has more scenes of systolic action than any other of Hemingway's novels. And each of these scenes is painted with a masterly hand, offering the minutest detail. Smells of all kind, various hues and shades of human skin, contours of the muscle and the movement of the body, the richness of the sun and the sky, the physical appetite for food, the physical appetite for sexual gratification, the physical fears, of death, of survival, are all registered with tremendous force and accuracy, and the novel does show that Hemingway was an artist immensely sensitive to the physical world around him, and shows how much delight he took in the day-to-day living of that world.

But along with that we have also to see that Robert Jordan is not quite contented with the physical; he is eternally disturbed. It is all right to be able to handle your gun with accuracy or to be able to distinguish virtues of horses at a glance, but is that all that there is to life? We never see Kashkin in the story, but every now and then his name is cleverly brought up by Hemingway to provide us with a counterpart to Robert Jordan. Though members of the Pablo gang think Robert Jordan to be very different from Kashkin, Robert Jordan and Kashkin are in reality two different sides of the same personality. Kashkin is what Robert Jordan used to be at one time or would still like to be; Kashkin is Jake Barnes of *The Sun Also Rises* or Frederick Henry of *A Farewell to Arms*. From what we gather from the descriptions of Pablo and his guerrillas, he was a sensitive man, reticent in speech and somewhat nervous in bearing. Though he was very brave, he was also afraid at heart and remained aloof from others and spoke in a strange manner.

Strangely, that is how Robert Jordan strikes us too. Except that he has trained himself by now not to give his innermost thoughts away. His shooting of Kashkin appears to me to be symbolic of his shooting of his own old self. Kashkin was too "jumpy" for a revolutionary. He was a little "crazy." In this business, you have to learn to be "very cold in the head." Agustín evidently is right when he tells Jordan: "You look like the other one. . . . But something different."[6] Thus Robert Jordan and Kashkin are the same individual. Only Jordan has purposely closed the door on his other self. Through a supreme effort of will, he succeeds in keeping that door closed throughout the novel.

But we should make no mistake about it. Robert Jordan's heart is not in the war; he has constantly to remind himself of it to remain in tune with it. Already, when the story opens, he is beginning to lose his memory connected with the war. He cannot recall the name of Anselmo when he meets him and this worries him; he considers it a "bad sign."[7] There are "other things" too about which he worries, though they remain unspecified.[8] By the end of the day he concedes to himself that he is getting "gloomy"; "the job had overwhelmed him a little. Slightly overwhelmed, he thought. Plenty overwhelmed."[9]

Why these alarming signs, particularly when he knows of his dexterity with his hands and knows also that he has been doing sabotage work for quite some time? The answer to the query is that his essential preoccupations are elsewhere. He is not a soldier by temperament. By temperament, he is an aesthete, a lover of beauty; a sensitive human concerned with such subtle thoughts as immortality or love or death. His lengthy dialogue with Anselmo on the subject of killing is very revealing. He is not really for killing at all; left to himself he would not kill even animals. "But I feel nothing against it when it is necessary. When it is for the cause."[10] It is the old man Anselmo who is the more articulate in this conversation; it is he who says that "to take the life of another is to me very grave," it is a "sin"; but Robert Jordan seems to agree with him. Both of them justify or condone killing only in terms of the present necessity forced by the civil war, by "the cause." "That bridge can be the point on which the future of the human race can turn. As it can turn on everything that happens in this war."[11] Again Jordan reminds himself that he has only to do his duty and not to think of anything else. His main concern is only "one"—the bridge. "You have only one thing to do and you must do it," he tells himself. "Only one thing, hell, he thought. If it were one thing it was easy. Stop worrying, you windy bastard, he said to himself. Think about something else."[12] Repeatedly he tells himself in the story, "You are a bridge-blower now. Not a thinker." But it does not help.

The subject of killing is posed frequently in *For Whom the Bell Tolls*, including the lengthy account of killings that Pilar gives—first the killings done by Pablo and then by her other lover, Finito, in the bullring. But at least on two other occasions Hemingway examines the subject in its moral implications (in addition to the present one in chapter 3). In chapter 15, the day after the earlier discussion with Robert Jordan, Anselmo once again goes over the whole question. And again he cannot justify the killing of other human beings.

> I think that after the war there will have to be . . . great penance done for the killing. If we no longer have religion after the war then I think there must be some form of civic penance organized that all may be cleansed from the killing or else we will never have a true and human basis for living.[13]

In chapter 26, we return to the subject. This time it is Robert Jordan, at another part of the scene on the same day. El Sordo is being attacked by a column of cavalry and is being bombed out of his position by planes. Robert Jordan is going through the documents found on the body of the cavalryman whom he had shot dead in the morning. A part of his self is uneasy, and is nagging him with: "Do you think you have a right to kill any one?"[14] He goes round and round and tries to get rid of the irritating worry. At the same time, in the distance, he can see El Sordo and his party, his own companions, being wiped out by fascists. Robert Jordan is in a truly diastolic mood here, and he is open to several forces beyond his comprehension which are swaying him at the moment. A part of his self, the systolic part, the part depending on "action," tries to justify the killing. But the diastolic mood is strong enough for him to admit:

> But you mustn't believe in killing, he told himself. You must do it as a necessity but you must not believe in it. If you believe in it the whole thing is wrong.[15]

In none of Hemingway's novels does the hero talk so much with himself as in *For Whom the Bell Tolls*—an indication enough of his inner conflict and disturbance.

> Listen, he told himself. You better cut this out. This is very bad for you and for your work. Then himself said back to him, You listen, see? Because you are doing something very serious and I have to see you understand it all the time. I have to keep you straight in your head. Because if you are not absolutely straight in your head you have no right to do the things you do for all of them are crimes and no man has a right to take another man's life unless it is to prevent something worse happening to other people. So get it straight and do not lie to yourself.[16]

The passage is typical of the way Robert Jordan's two halves try to win him over. Just as in Harry of "The Snows of Kilimanjaro," the two moods, systolic and diastolic, are openly recorded by Hemingway, so too in Robert Jordan the two moods openly prevail. "Said he to himself." "Himself said back to him." That is how it goes most of the time.

So we must notice that Robert Jordan's life of action—the many things that he "does" in a systolic fashion—does not imply an essential shift in the Hemingway hero. The Hemingway hero continues to be a spontaneous and a passive individual. Anselmo is baffled at this apparent contradiction in Robert Jordan. For the "Inglés" talks of killing and action, and "yet he seems to be both sensitive and kind."[17] But the contradiction is resolved when we see that Robert Jordan's present activity is the result of the ideology to which he seems to be temporarily committed. Temperamentally he does not want that kind of life.

> Well, I don't want to be a soldier, he thought. I know that. So that's out.[18]

And this is where the love story in the novel plays a vital part in revealing to us the true nature of the hero. What Maria does to Robert Jordan is to make a man of him once again—the basic man that he was before he got involved with the civil war. All his responses up to the point where he finds Maria show that Robert Jordan has become more a robot than a man; he has become someone who lives on the clichés of his new-found ideology. He must have repeated these clichés to himself time and time again, and must finally have convinced himself of their value, notwithstanding his natural impulse to the contrary. The result is that he is now only an "instrument" to do his "duty."[19] "Thou art very religious about thy politics,"[20] Pilar tells him teasingly, but he accepts it as a compliment and does not laugh. Later when she asks him seriously if he has no fears in life, his reply is: "Only of not doing my duty as I should":

> "You are a very cold boy."
> "No," he said. "I do not think so."
> "No. In the head you are very cold."
> "It is that I am very preoccupied with my work."
> "But you do not like the things of life?"
> "Yes. Very much. But not to interfere with my work."

"You like to drink, I know. I have seen."

"Yes. Very much. But not to interfere with my work."

"And women?"

"I like them very much, but I have not given them much importance."[21]

This is how he is until he has consummated his love with Maria; an automaton, who has willed himself to a life of ideology. The ideology remains till the end. But with the arrival of Maria in his life, he begins seeing it for what it is worth and begins recovering his own, original self.

That was one thing that sleeping with Maria had done. He had gotten to be as bigoted and hidebound about his politics as a hard-shelled Baptist and phrases like enemies of the people came into his mind without his much criticizing them in any way. Any sort of *clichés* both revolutionary and patriotic. His mind employed them without criticism. Of course they were true but it was too easy to be nimble about using them. But since last night and this afternoon his mind was much clearer and cleaner on that business.[22]

What his original self wants is peace of mind rather than valor. Maria makes him see this clearly:

So far she had not affected his resolution but he would much prefer not to die. He would abandon a hero's or a martyr's end gladly. He did not want to make a Thermopylae, nor be Horatius at any bridge, nor be the Dutch boy with his finger in that dyke. No. He would like to spend some time with Maria. That was the simplest expression of it. He would like to spend a long, long time with her.[23]

It could be Jake Barnes or Frederick Henry speaking. Not every man a piece of the Continent, "because I am involved in Mankinde," but "private peace."

iii

In the matter of structure again the difficulties that *For Whom the Bell Tolls* presents are only surface difficulties.

But let us look at those difficulties. First of all, the story is told from the point of view of omniscience, where the author can at his convenience see everything and present whatever he wants to the reader. Carlos Baker has spoken of the "epic" quality of *For Whom the Bell Tolls*.[24] A story narrated from the standpoint of omniscience has much to do with that impression. For it gives the novelist a wider scope and he can fill in a much bigger canvas. He can then paint a civilization rather than a few characters and their destiny. But with all the advantages that such a method offers, the epic mode is not experimental in nature and there is very little that the novelist can do through it that has not been tried before. Further, with our current disregard of the epic as a genre of literature, with our interest more in the individual than in the race, it is doubtful if *For Whom the Bell Tolls* would emerge a successful novel if it were to be viewed only as an epic. (To say nothing of the doubtful nature of the validity of the Spanish scene captured by the novel as an epic, about which Spanish critics of this novel like Arturo Barea have expressed definite reservations.[25])

Another structural difficulty that gets in our way is that in point of fact *For Whom the Bell Tolls* is not one story but several put together. The novel does have a central plot, the blowing up of the bridge, but there are other stories independent of the bridge, narrated at considerable length and with considerable interest by the novelist. We are not here speaking of subplots, for subplots are in some manner connected with the main plot and do not constitute a separate section. The story of Maria, for instance—

her early life and what happened to her before she met Robert Jordan—cannot be considered as a separate story because her fate is ultimately linked up with Robert Jordan and her earlier life merely becomes a subplot of the main plot. But there are stories in *For Whom the Bell Tolls* which have nothing to do with the main plot and are independent of it.

Mainly, there are three distinct stories in *For Whom the Bell Tolls* which have no true bearing on each other. First, there is the story of Robert Jordan and Maria. Then we have the story of Pilar and Pablo. Last, there is the story of the Russians, which includes men like Golz, Kleber, Hans, André Marty and Karkov (complete with a wife and a mistress). Or, if we prefer plot to character, we may say that there are the story of the bridge, the story of the cave, and the story of the plain, with Gaylord ("the hotel in Madrid the Russians had taken over") as the nerve center of that plain.

Though Hemingway tries to reconcile the three stories, and a loose relationship among them is established, they are really three separate stories, with a separate set of people, a separate locale, and a separate motivating force. The result is that it becomes almost an unwieldy problem for the novelist, as far as structure. In the course of his writing career, Hemingway tried that experiment twice: in *To Have and Have Not* (where there are two distinct stories, the story of Harry and Marie Morgan and the story of Richard and Helen Gordon) and in *For Whom the Bell Tolls*. And both times, it damages the tight systolic-diastolic pattern that one observes in Hemingway's other novels.

But Hemingway does not abandon the pattern. If anything, he extends it, and tries to maintain the systolic-diastolic structure in each of the separate stories within the novel. The monologues of Marie Morgan, and some of the scenes between Richard and Helen Gordon are indicative of the caesuras, the diastolic pauses in the separate stories in *To Have and Have Not*. The same is true of *For Whom the Bell Tolls*. Both these novels consequently become novels of multiple systoles and multiple diastoles—and thereby of multiple caesuras. But Hemingway does not quite succeed in coordinating the various systole-diastoles effectively.

The main story in *For Whom the Bell Tolls* is of Robert Jordan and Maria, and the perceptive reader can see the continuation of the systolic-diastolic stance in that principal tale; activity and inactivity alternate throughout in what they do. Let us take note here of one of the other stories, and see how the method works there.

The story of Pablo and Pilar is a masterpiece of love-hate relationship, and these characters are undoubtedly two of the finest drawn by Hemingway. Pablo is in command when the novel opens. When it closes, he is again in command. He is supposed to be the bad type of guerrilla leader, El Sordo the good. But in guerrilla warfare, what matters is not morality but cunning. Pablo is the sharper of the two men, quicker to grasp a situation, better in strategy, better in tactics too. He is also more vicious, less humane, and more foul-mouthed. One imagines the two to be equally brave. We see El Sordo in action, when his camp is surrounded by the carbineers. But Pilar's account of Pablo in action, when under his command the guerrillas took over a certain town, shows him to be just as brave. In addition, Pablo has cunning, which El Sordo lacks. When it will serve his cunning, he is willing to let the leadership of the band pass on to Pilar. When it will serve his cunning, he can murder in cold blood some of his own companions (after the attack on the bridge). On balance, he is in all probability a better guerrilla leader than El Sordo.

But more fascinating than his role as a guerrilla leader is the play of emotion between him and Pilar. They certainly are bound to each other, on some occasions in love, on others in hatred. The extent of the bond between them is well illustrated when Pablo returns to the cave, first having deserted the place with some of Robert Jordan's equipment. The detonators from Jordan's bag are gone and gone along with them is Pablo. But early in the morning he reappears at the mouth of the cave, and everyone is struck dumb. Robert Jordan thinks that perhaps he has had a moment of remorse, for he has just told Jordan that he has brought back with him five men—men from the bands of Elias and Alejandro (the men he was to murder later). But no, Pablo has not suffered any pangs of conscience; he has not come back for the sake of Robert Jordan. He has returned for the sake of Pilar. The innocence and the abruptness with which he accepts this is touching. He is a big, murderous man. But he is bound inextricably to that ugly and passionate female, Pilar.

"I am glad to see thee," Robert Jordan said. He walked over to him. "We are all right with the grenades. That will work . . ."

"Nay," Pablo said. "I do nothing for thee. Thou are a thing of bad omen. All of this comes from thee. Sordo also. But after I had thrown away thy material I found myself too lonely."

"Thy mother—" Pilar said.[26]

By Pablo's admission, he returns because he missed Pilar and was feeling lonely. And this after an absence of only a few hours! The entire scene that follows is remarkable in its diastolic grandeur. Pilar and Pablo had quarreled earlier, too; in the novel there is the scene where she openly defies him and takes over the command of the band. One has the feeling that perhaps she secretly wished his death and would have sanctioned it if Jordan had gone that far. But that was at the systolic level. On the other hand, their expressions of attachment to each other are equally pronounced, but these come at strange moments and are not so openly displayed. When Pablo leaves this night with the stuff from Robert Jordan's bag, he knows he is leaving for good. Tomorrow is the day when the bridge is to be blown, and if he disappears the night before with the valuable explosives, he knows that Pilar will never forgive him. He thus knows that his break with Pilar is a final one this time, and that he cannot come back.

It is the diastolic realization of this that does things to him. After he threw away the vital equipment "down the gorge into the river," the systolic part of the action came to an end. It is then that he senses the finality of his break with Pilar. In the diastolic mood that follows (of which we know only after his arrival back at the cave), he is driven by forces beyond his control to work somehow for his reacceptance back at the camp. It is the diastolic energy that sends him up to Elias and Alejandro for men to help in the bridge assignment. It is the diastolic energy that makes him confess his need for Pilar the moment he gets back inside the cave.

And the response of Pilar is as touching. She banters with him and scoffs at him for his cowardice, but inwardly she is happy.

Then to Pablo, her eyes softening. "So you have come back, eh?"

"Yes, woman," Pablo said.

"Well, thou art welcome," Pilar said to him. "I did not think thou couldst be the ruin thou appeared to be."

"Having done such a thing there is a loneliness that cannot be borne," Pablo said to her quietly.

"That cannot be borne," she mocked him. "That cannot be borne by thee for fifteen minutes."

"Don't mock me, woman. I have come back."[27]

Pilar's feelings are mixed, as indeed are Pablo's. Their sense of the cowardly thing he did is a part of the total makeup of the moment. But their sense of mutual need of each other is also a part of the content.

In the end we read:

"Thou," she said and her husky voice was fond again. "Thou. I suppose if a man has something once, always something of it remains."

"*Listo,*" Pablo said, looking at her squarely and flatly now. "I am ready for what the day brings."

"I believe thou art back," Pilar said to him. "I believe it. But, *hombre,* thou wert a long way gone."[28]

Scenes of diastolic significance between the two also appear much earlier in the novel. In fact, right from the start we observe the curious attachment with which they are bound to each other. The day after Pilar has nominally taken command of the band, Robert Jordan finds her in a particularly sad mood. He suggests, it "will dissipate as the sun rises. It is like a mist."[29] Pilar quietly accepts that explanation, but then goes on to tell him of the real reason. A few minutes back she has been unfair to Pablo in the cave. She had narrated to his face her fondness for his rival, the bullfighter Finito, with who she had earlier lived, and her gay adventures with him in the city of Valencia. This had wounded Pablo and it is the thought of that which is making Pilar sad—"I wounded him much with the story. Kill him, yes. Curse him, yes. But wound him, no."[30]

The conversation between Robert Jordan and Pilar that morning takes place in the diastolic phase, the phase of the pause after the stormy systolic scene of the last night. Last night, standing firmly on her feet and holding her big cooking spoon as a baton, she had told Pablo: "Listen to me, drunkard. You understand who commands here? . . . Listen well. I command."[31] But that part of the tension is over now and has generated instead a diastolic mood of solitude and sorrow.

Pilar and Robert Jordan are getting ready to leave for the camp of El Sordo and Pablo has gone off to the corral to see to the horses. Robert Jordan looks at her as she stands before him, "the big, brown-faced woman with her kind, widely set eyes and her square, heavy face, lined and pleasantly ugly, the eyes merry, but the face sad until the lips moved."[32] Pilar is perhaps the finest female character drawn by Hemingway, perfect within the dimensions he allows her. She is a rough peasant woman, and like a true peasant her beauty and charm lie not in her looks but in the vigor of her body and in the compassion of her understanding—even though on surface she sounds rough and vulgar.

The conversation that now takes place between Jordan and Pilar is given in a slower, pensive rhythm and the scene is that of diastolic caesura, one of the pauses in the story of Pablo and Pilar. Pilar's concern for Pablo is so genuine that Robert Jordan is moved by her artlessness, and in a fit of impulsiveness (he does not provide us with many such occasions) he throws his arms around her and says, "I care for thee, too . . . I care for thee very much."[33]

In this conversation Pilar also tells us that Pablo had been crying last night. Imagine Pablo crying! That is what the impact of a major piece of diastolic action does to a Hemingway character; that is what a caesura implies —the sudden cessation of the normal course of the story. Pablo's character as delineated for us earlier in the novel has in it no place for tears. He is a guerrilla leader, a professional killer. But now he has been overthrown in his own camp, and by none other than his own *mujer*, his own wife. This brings in new awarenesses and he cries hideously, "in a short and ugly manner as a man cries when it is as though there is an animal inside that is shaking him."[34]

That must have been a moment of powerful diastolic reality, but Hemingway does not expand it for us. But as the story proceeds, there comes another major caesura in the narrative, another major diastolic scene in the forward movement of the novel.

This time the pause concerns Pilar alone, but it is meant to convey the complexity of her personal life and her relationship with Pablo, for the scene takes us straight into her heart. We know from Maria that it was Pilar who had sent her to sleep with Robert Jordan. She had been sorry at what the girl had gone through at the hands of the fascists, and like a watchdog she had for some time protected her from the men of her own group. But when Jordan arrives on the scene, she offers her to him as a beloved.

One imagines that she did this as therapy for poor Maria; she never expected the deep love that springs up between Robert Jordan and Maria. Sensitive and intuitive as she is, she soon notices the presence of that something bigger than life between them. This in a strange way hurts her and accentuates for her her own ugliness. Not that men had not wanted her when she was in her prime. She knows that and is proud of it; occasion permitting, she is willing to talk of that openly. But no one wants her now except this brute Pablo, who, slowly turning coward, is concerned more with questions of safety than with love and adventure.

Even in this analysis, we are going too far. The whole point of Hemingway's technique is that he does not make things quite so explicit. The fact is that somehow the love between Robert Jordan and Maria hurts Pilar. In what manner it hurts, or what exactly is the area of her hurt and need, is made clear only indirectly. It is like Pablo's crying in the night, or like Pablo's returning to the cave the night after he deserts camp. In those cases too, the reaction of the moment is not explicitly stated. Hemingway is more concerned with the complexity of diastolic response which defies human attitudinizing.

So the next morning, when Pilar questions Maria and Robert Jordan about what they did in the night and neither one gives her a straight answer and each is purposely evasive, she senses the fullness of their relationship. And while traveling to the camp of El Sordo, walking on foot, the diastolic mood comes upon her and she is a different Pilar.

She sits down by the side of a stream and wants to rest. Robert Jordan urges her to hurry along but she pays no heed. Rather, she takes off her shoes and puts her feet into the water. Deep in the diastolic reflex, she then goes on to give a pretty little speech on the nature and quality of love to Jordan and Maria. "Life is very curious. . . . I would have made a good man, but I am all woman and all ugly. Yet many men have loved me and I have loved many men. . . ."[35]

The time and the occasion of the scene must be observed. They have an urgent mission to perform; there is a civil war on. But Pilar is powerless—she can only surrender herself to the diastolic mood.

In the reminiscent, sad attitude that that mood generates, she gives a long account of an attack on a certain city when Pablo had distinguished himself by his physical courage, and when there was much killing. This long account and the note on which it ends—the note which speaks of Pablo's telling her that night, "Pilar, tonight we will do nothing"—makes one sense that she is narrating the story not for the benefit of Robert Jordan or Maria but for her own. Even though she calls it the "worst day" of her life, she is in point of fact reliving a love story— her own love story, with the then-brave Pablo. The dominant mood of the moment is one of sadness, expressive of her present sorrow that she is now old and ugly and unwanted.

In the afternoon, on their return journey after the conference with El Sordo, we once again become aware that Pilar is being consumed by a private sorrow. Robert Jordan finds that her "brown face looked pallid and the skin sallow and that there were dark areas under her eyes."[36] Yet, this time it is she who is against sitting down and resting, though both Robert Jordan and Maria have asked her to. She is even irritable, and abruptly tells Maria, "Shut up. . . . Nobody asked for thy advice."[37] But she relents and finally does sit down under a pine tree. She apologizes to Maria for being rude to her, and acknowledges clearly, "I don't know what has held me today."[38] Through such developments, Hemingway is giving expression to the same, unanalyzable, dark, diastolic forces that surround all of us in life and certainly surround most of his characters. Pilar since morning has become a different woman, and she does not quite know why.

They are sitting on a mountain slope and in the distance they can see snow shining on the mountain peaks.

"What rotten stuff is the snow and how beautiful it looks," Pilar said. "What an illusion is the snow." She turned to Maria. "I am sorry I was rude to thee, *guapa*. I don't know what has held me today. I have an evil temper."

"I never mind what you say when you are angry," Maria told her. "And you are angry often."

"Nay, it is worse than anger," Pilar said, looking across at the peaks.

"Thou art not well," Maria said.

"Neither is it that," the woman said.[39]

It is an extremely subtle passage, indicative of Hemingway's genius at communicating the force of the diastolic action. The ignorant peasant woman is today talking of "illusions" and "reality," herself only half aware of what is passing through her. And yet the reader is left in no doubt about the enormous storm or turmoil brewing within. She herself can sense that it is not just anger, or ill health—it is something more than that. But Hemingway does not objectify her feelings beyond that point.

However, we see that soon she returns to the subject of the passion between Robert Jordan and Maria. At this stage comes the startling admission, all of a sudden and almost involuntarily, that what has been bothering Pilar is plain jealousy. "I am jealous and say it and it is there. And I say it."[40] Maria is shocked and tells her not to utter such things. But that has little effect on Pilar and she goes on uncontrollably to tell Jordan that he has eaten Maria's tongue, for Maria has suddenly gone quiet. Then she chides him for calling Maria "rabbit" and in a way seems to resent that, too. Jordan tells her that she is a very "hard" woman, and Pilar answers back, "No . . . But so simple I am very complicated." Throughout the exchange that follows, sexual symbols are uppermost in Pilar's mind and once again she asserts, "I am not much like myself today. . . . Very little like myself."[41]

And then, as though further to confirm her knowledge of the love between the young couple, and, by implication, further to torture herself about her own ugliness and old age and her present physical relationship with Pablo, she offers to leave Jordan and Maria together behind in the woods to do what she grossly calls "that." There was no special need for her to do this; Jordan and Maria did not want "that" at this time, at least not to begin with, though once the subject is broached Maria urges Jordan to let Pilar go ahead alone. But Pilar does this for her own sake, to satisfy the new demon in herself, the diastolic demon.

The end of this diastolic scene is reached when Jordan and Maria catch up with her after their love-making. We see Pilar reduced to a helpless bundle in her consciousness of her present neglect. Jordan and Maria see her from a distance, and approach her:

"Who is that?" Robert Jordan asked and pointed.

"Pilar," the girl said, looking along his arm. "Surely it is Pilar."

At the lower edge of the meadow where the first trees grew the woman was sitting, her head on her arms. She looked like a dark bundle from where they stood; black against the brown of the tree trunk.

"Come on," Robert Jordan said and started to run toward her through the knee-high heather. It was heavy and hard to run in and when he had run a little way, he slowed and walked. He could see the woman's head was on her folded arms and she looked broad and black against the tree trunk. He came up to her and said, "Pilar!" sharply.

The woman raised her head and looked up at him.
"Oh," she said. "You have terminated already?"[42]

The validity of strange, dark forces of life that are not open to rationalization and yet are ever present around man, is repeatedly established in Hemingway's fiction. In the story of Pilar and Pablo in *For Whom the Bell Tolls,* the narrative follows the curve of physical action and then dips into those inexplicable mysteries which surround the path of direct action. Pilar starts off on a solid note in the book, when we meet her first inside the cave. But in the course of the story, the diastolic realization comes upon her and she is no longer sure of herself. Her tactless remarks to Maria and Jordan, and her insistence on knowing from them how the sexual act had gone between them, seem foolish. But they are only an indication of her helplessness before the new urges that have seized her. Jordan and Maria have made her realize many things that must forever remain beyond the scope of rational comprehension. Jordan and Maria were not a conscious instrument of the diastolic change; they were not even aware of what they were doing to Pilar. The change, the realization, that comes about in Pilar is of its own making, dependent on the total impact of a given moment. It is a change which in a way baffles the individual.

iv

Just as the story of Pilar and Pablo begins on a systolic note and then proceeds through diastolic pauses, the other two stories in *For Whom the Bell Tolls,* the story of Robert Jordan and Maria and the story of the Russians, also begin on the systolic note and are interspersed with diastolic moods. The character of each of the individuals involved in these stories is discovered only in the diastolic pause. It is in that pause, or a series of them, that Robert Jordan and Maria realize themselves and attain fulfillment. Throughout the novel there are multiple caesuras where they enlarge their comprehension of themselves through the diastolic revelation. The same is true of other characters. Repeatedly Hemingway uses a similar method in each case, as in that of El Sordo (pp. 309-10), of Lieutenant Berrendo (pp. 326-27), of Andrés (pp. 363-68), and of Comrade André Marty (pp. 422-24), where, on the pages referred to, these characters are in a state of relative diastole. The story of Robert Jordan and Maria, of course, constantly depends on that structure for its development and effect.

We shall now consider briefly Hemingway's mystic vision, or the mystic vision of his heroes. It may sound odd to speak of Hemingway as a "mystic." In his long life we do not find a trace of any such involvement. How then can we speak of his "mysticism"?

By mysticism we do not mean here esoteric practices or faiths; the term suggests rather an unverbalized awareness of something other than the physical life of man, awareness of what has been called earlier the larger life of the universe. It will here be worthwhile to stress a point of similarity between Hemingway and D. H. Lawrence: their intuitive acceptance of the mystic "other." In both novelists the reader is acutely aware of that other force, which runs parallel to and delimits the life of man. The difference is that in the case of Lawrence there is a total alignment with that mystic force, whereas in Hemingway the element of scepticism never leaves the author. The result is that whereas Lawrence's mystic vision is all too apparent on the very first reading of his novels, in Hemingway the reader is not likely to find any pronounced assertion of it. Lawrence accepted the religious basis of life and proceeded to build his stories on that fundamental assumption. In Hemingway there is doubt—and this doubt is apt to confuse the reader.

But basically Hemingway is as religious an artist as Lawrence. Both were against dogmatic religions, particularly institutionalized religions, and both depended more on intuition than on reason or intellect. Both had great faith in and wanted to celebrate the life of the senses.

As it happens, in *For Whom the Bell Tolls* Hemingway does formulate his religious vision. In his earlier work, we could only infer that vision, but in *For Whom the Bell Tolls*, there is an attempt made by him at formal theorizing as well.

We see this vision through the mind of Robert Jordan. As in Lawrence, in Hemingway the essential nature of the mystic vision comprehends and glorifies the force of the living moment, the present. There are innumerable passages in the novel which extol the virtue of that entity— the living moment. "If there is not any such thing as a long time, nor the rest of your lives, nor from now on, but there is only now, why then now is the thing to praise and I am very happy with it. Now, *ahora, maintenant, heute. Now*, it has a funny sound to be a whole world and your life."[43] In the same chapter, a few pages later, we find: "There is nothing else than now. There is neither yesterday, certainly, nor is there any tomorrow. How old must you be before you know that? There is only now, and if now is only two days, then two days is your life and everything in it will be in proportion."[44] There are other references in the novel with a similar intent.

These passages could easily be interpreted to mean Hemingway's preoccupation with the life of action—the day-to-day life of physical activity. But their mystical quality is seen in the fact that Robert Jordan utters the words (to himself), not in the context of his official duty of the blowing up of the bridge, but in the context of Maria and what Maria has brought to him. It has been an enormous experience, knowing her physically, and he had neither wanted nor anticipated the extreme reaction that it provoked. "I did not know that I could ever feel what I have felt, he thought."[45] Most of these lines are from chapter 13, one of the finest chapters of diastolic pauses in the novel. It is the chapter in which Pilar leaves Robert Jordan and Maria alone in the woods and walks ahead on their way back from El Sordo's camp. It is the chapter in which the earth "moves" after the sexual union, and in which Pilar is later discovered bowed over in a "bundle," immersed in her own diastolic awareness of boredom, jealousy, and disappointment.

Extremely romantic though the love between Jordan and Maria is, and doubtful though it may be that they could have continued that life of togetherness at the same pitch once the war was over and peace established, the value of the experience lies in the motivation imagined by each to lie behind it. Strangely enough, each, in his own separate way, considers this as a "religious" coming together. For both the desire was spontaneous. Says Maria: "I loved you when I saw you today and I loved you always but I never saw you before. . . ."[46] Confesses Robert Jordan: "You were gone when you first saw her. When she first opened her mouth and spoke to you it was there already and you know it."[47] But an even more important aspect of the relationship is the spiritual meaning they try to attach to it.

While lying with Robert Jordan the first time, Maria tells him of how things were done to her by the fascists, when she had fallen into their hands. Then with utter simplicity she confesses to him what Pilar had told her. "She said that nothing is done to oneself that one does not accept and that if I loved some one it would take it all away."[48] The poor girl has thus come to him with this faith and hope. She had wanted the act of love to be a benign force of renewal, a highly religious sentiment to say the least. It is with the same naïve faith and with the same urgency that she urges him, a little while later, "And now let us do quickly what it is we do so that the other is all gone."[49]

Robert Jordan is not overtly religious or vocal, as she is. But he is as sharply conscious of something new that has happened in his life, and on the day that they are going to blow up the bridge, the admission comes from him too that it was an experience which was "given" to him—given by an external spiritual power as an act of grace. He could not have projected it through an act of will; in fact he did not believe in the experience of love. But now it had come his way and had enriched him beyond anything earlier known by him. "In the last few days he had learned that he himself, with another person, could be everything." He adds: "That was given to me, perhaps, because I never asked for it. That cannot be taken away nor lost."[50]

It is the mystic, "given" nature of the experience that determines the religious quality of the relationship. The bridge finally is blown up, and Robert Jordan is going to die. It is then that what he has discovered through dia-stolic revelations becomes truly pronounced. For he shows an inner strength in the last scene not apparent in him in the early sections of the novel. Quite convincingly he assures Maria that that is not the end. He tells her that if one of them continues to live, then both of them live on. "As long as there is one of us there is both of us."[51] He tells her "I am thee," and "Thou art me too now," and speaks of "The me in thee." The only time we have seen identical language in Hemingway is when Catherine professes her love for Frederick Henry in *A Farewell to Arms*. But it is unusual language for a Hemingway hero.

One could perhaps say that the expressions are the result of the exigencies of the moment. Robert Jordan wants Maria to leave, and there is no other way of persuading her except through semi-religious, mystical invocations of this type. This is partly true, as Jordan himself suspects. But there is an equally powerful assertion by him of the new faith. He tells himself:

> Try to believe what you told her. That is the best. And who says it is not true? Not you. You don't say it, any more than you would say the things did not happen that happened. Stay with what you believe now. Don't get cynical.[52]

The presence of a new faith is clear from the words: "Stay with what you believe now." There has been a transformation, as indeed there was in the other Hemingway heroes. But Robert Jordan ends as the least cynical of them all.

This leads me to conclude that the epigraph from Donne, "No man is an Iland, intire of it selfe," has its implications more in an extension of the individual toward a mystical union with the cosmos, with created life in general, than in an extension toward the individual's societal obligations. Hemingway certainly wanted to portray societal obligations, for the same epigraph from Donne has also the words, "because I am involved in Mankinde." But on the way, a different kind of affirmation came to the fore. Robert Jordan has acquitted himself well as a soldier of the Republic, and he can die with satisfaction on that score. But the important affirmation in the novel is not of what the Republic stands for. The important affirmation is of the fact that in life no single line of thought or approach is right. To me the most important lines in the entire novel are when Robert Jordan, minutes away from death, asserts: "There's *no* one thing that's true. It's all true."[53] He is lying in a state of passivity, utterly in the grip of a diastolic pause. He is sorry that he is going to die, for life is so plentiful and he will be taken away from it. But then he rebukes himself:

> You've had as good a life as any one because of these last days. You do not want to complain when you have been so lucky. I wish there was some way to pass on what I've learned, though. Christ, I was learning fast there at the end.[54]

The gist of what he has learned is the two lines quoted above: "There's *no* one thing that's true. It's all true." For in the next line, Robert Jordan, looking at the fields stretched before him and thinking of the tension between the rival military groups, notices "the way the planes are beautiful whether they are ours or theirs."

These are essentially religious assertions, speaking of the totality of life; it is difficult to find another expression for them. *For Whom the Bell Tolls* thereby is Hemingway's valuable doctrinal assertion of the beauty and the complexity of life (even though it is not his best novel). Life is beautiful, no matter what the impediments. Life is beautiful, no matter what the challenges. The challenges and the impediments rather highlight the extreme subtlety of this elusive thing called life. There is nothing else that can match that subtlety. There is nothing else that can replace it. Robert Jordan was vaguely aware of it when the novel opened. Now, at its end, he willingly accepts that faith.

6

Across the River and Into the Trees

i

Hemingway's ultimate moment of triumph as an artist arrives with his last novel, *The Old Man and the Sea*, published in 1952. It is in that novel that we have the gigantic sweep of his genius, which stretches upward and beyond, and gives us an intense presentation of the contraries of life, unsullied by personal despair. There are no *nadas* in that novel. There is no heavy drinking; there is no drinking at all. There is no sex there, either. There is no social obligation as such. Further, there are no expressions of nihilism such as are present in much of Hemingway's earlier fiction. On the other hand, his last novel is the most complete assertion of total life that ever came from his pen.

But before dealing with it, we should take brief note of *Across the River and Into the Trees*. Pressed to do so, a Hemingway admirer could perhaps make a case for it as a genuine Hemingway novel. Indeed, the structure of the novel is typically Hemingwayan; there are moments of action and, interspersed, many diastolic pauses in the story when the protagonist, Colonel Cantwell, is carried further into his own knowledge of himself and the life around him. But one feature that marks any genuine creative effort is missing here—inventiveness. The novel has very little of invention in it. The endless listing of places where Colonel Cantwell has fought in the first war, and the long accounts of what he did in the second, an account narrated to Countess Renata, is too factual to be interesting fictionally; it runs like an inventory and never quite takes off at the level of the imagination.

It is easier to accept *Across the River and Into the Trees* as part of Hemingway's nonfiction, along with *Green Hills of Africa* and *Death in the Afternoon*. There is some interesting characterization in it, as in those two books. There are some interesting episodes as well, as, again, we find in the two earlier volumes of nonfiction. But it is hard to place the book alongside Hemingway's fiction. For once, Hemingway seems to have ignored his own rule of craftsmanship: not to confuse creative writing with journalism. There is very little in the novel that is truly "made up." To repeat what has already been quoted, Hemingway believed (and rightly) that the process of creation presupposed a departure from the actual physical happening. To quote Hemingway: "If you make it up instead of describe it you can make it round and whole and solid and give it life." That kind of creativity is absent in *Across the River and Into the Trees*.

And then, the novel is also a sad case of the legend's catching up with the man. Over the years, Hemingway's reputation had grown. In the posthumously published *A Moveable Feast*, we see Hemingway as a poor foreigner in Paris back in 1920s. His principal aim then was to write, and if he associated with anyone it was with writers (most of the portraits in *A Moveable Feast* are of fellow writers). But now, after the second war, Hemingway was living in grand style in "the Finca" in Cuba, and Malcolm Cowley, Lilian Ross, and Hotchner had appeared on the scene to paint not so much a hard-working writer as a hard-living virile man. Hemingway liked that image—the "Capitano" figure—and had always secretly longed for it. The second world war offered a suitable opportunity, and we read in the account of his life how first he organized an anti-submarine patrol in the Gulf Stream with himself in the role of captain, and later, in Europe, once actually took command and directed operations in a village near Paris (for which an explanation was asked of him later, as he had violated military rules).

When Hemingway the war correspondent returned to civil life after the second war, he continued to nourish that image. His letters to General Charles T. Lanham over the years, from 1944 to 1961, speak with nostalgic longing of the time that he had spent with his regiment. In 1945 he went as far as to write Lanham that he did not give a damn about writing and would rather be back with him. He added that the "goddam boring civil life" was wonderful but he was bored right through the marrow of all the old bones.[1] One notices in these letters, now in possession of the Princeton University library, with how much yearning Hemingway refers to his regiment, and the delight he gets in reliving old details like the Paris entry by the Allied troops. For years after the second war, he wrote nothing (*For Whom the Bell Tolls*, his last novel, was published in 1940), for he could not put between himself and his grandiose image of what he had done during the war a sufficient distance for his imagination to function. Finally he returned to writing. But although, when *Across the River and Into the Trees* appeared, he believed in it as a work of the imagination and wrote to General Lanham with much confidence that it had a hell of a man in it, a fine girl, and a good city and some country,[2] the work never achieves the intensity of his best earlier fiction.

What Hemingway does in *Across the River and Into the Trees* is to reenact for himself the second world war at the level of information. He fills it up with details that may satisfy the public image of him that had slowly been growing. The basic theme of the novel is delicate enough; the theme of death. The relationship of the Colonel with the young Renata is also delicately conceived, in that the vitality of the young girl could be used effectively to set off and further deepen the sorrow of age. But this delicate theme of age and death is not effectively developed. Neither is the presence of the driver Jackson or the duck-shooting scene—again indicative of youth and vitality—used by Hemingway to advantage. Both Jackson (in the first half of the book) and Renata (in the later half) are merely used by Hemingway to provide occasion for Colonel Cantwell to talk. The theme of both sections thus turns out to be, "I helped defend it" ("The Colonel, being then a Lieutenant"). There is not another piece of writing by Hemingway where the first-person pronoun is employed by him with such a vengeance. Renata is obviously in love with the Colonel (a love the origins of which are never explained) and she listens to his account ecstatically (chapters 29 through 33), but the driver, Jackson, is plainly sick, and there is an evident sting in his observation when the Colonel, having shown him a bridge and a house blown up during the war by medium bombers, goes on to draw a lesson for his benefit: "I guess the lesson is don't ever build yourself a country house. . . ." Jackson's crisp reply is: "I knew there must be a lesson in it, sir."[3] The Colonel is dead right when he informs Renata, "It is dull but it is informative."[4] The Colonel was being modest with her, or modestly vain, but that is how the novel actually strikes the reader: not quite dull all the time, but mostly "informative."

In another respect too one has the feeling that Hemingway was trying to project a predetermined image in this novel, rather than sensitively develop a given theme and situation. The novel was written in 1949; Hemingway's big wound in the first war had been received in 1918. More than thirty years had elapsed meanwhile, and the legend about the wound had now been given much prominence (by Hemingway personally and by his admirers). Certainly he must have relived that wound many times in his mind, and must have come to believe firmly in that wound and in his heroism—something that he did not believe in in 1918, or as late as 1929, when *A Farewell to Arms* came out. The result is that by the time *Across the River and Into the Trees* was written, the myth of that wound becomes the central image in the novel and destroys the creative force of the work.

In all probability, it was Hemingway himself who, with *Across the River and Into the Trees*, provided his critics with a ready metaphor to beat him with: the metaphor of the wound. The wounding of Frederick Henry in *A Farewell to Arms* is mentioned as an episode in the novel, never more than that; Frederick himself makes light of it when Rinaldi comes to see him, and narrates the unheroic circumstances in which he had been hit. Is there any other work of Hemingway in which the wound is developed or so morbidly referred to as in *Across the River and Into the Trees*? Is there any other work in which the protagonist so assiduously believes in the "merit" of that wound?

It begins early in *Across the River and Into the Trees*. The doctor asks the Colonel how many concussions he has had, injuries to the head. Frederick Henry would have laughed at such a question. But Colonel Cantwell replies seriously, "Maybe ten. . . . Give or take three."[5] The driver, Jackson, of course knows that "he's been beat up so much he's slug-nutty."[6] Then the Colonel moves in to enlighten us. He is thinking of the fight with the Austrians in 1918:

> He was hit three times that winter, but they were all gift wounds; small wounds in the flesh of the body without breaking bone, and he had become quite confident of his personal immortality since he knew he should have been killed in the heavy artillery bombardment that always preceded the attacks. Finally, he did get hit properly and for good. No one of his other wounds had ever done to him what the first big one did. I suppose it is just the loss of immortality, he thought. Well, in a way, that is quite a lot to lose.[7]

Two things are worth noticing about this passage. First of all, the Colonel in these words, "I suppose it is just the loss of immortality," is not speaking of a personal fear. Coming as it does after his reference to his earlier youthful boast about "immortality"—the confidence we all have when we are very young and immature—the second assertion is only registering the process of growing up, where, with the acquisition of experience, particularly the experience of being very close to death, Cantwell now no longer has his pig-headed belief in his imperishableness. The words, analyzed textually, do not mean the rise of fear in his mind.

Secondly, it is significant that it is only here that Hemingway speaks of the symbolic intent of a wound—not so much in sorrow as in sentimental attachment to that wound.

This is how the wounding account goes in *The Sun Also Rises.* "Well, it was a rotten way to be wounded and flying on a joke front like the Italian. In the Italian hos-

pital we were going to form a society."[8] That is all that
Hemingway says there. In *A Farewell to Arms*, the episode
starts with "Through the other noise I heard a cough,
then came the chuh-chuh-chuh-chuh—then there was a
flash, as when a blast-furnace door is swung open, and
a roar that started white and went red and on and on
in a rushing wind."[9] In the paragraph that follows, it is
the immediate feeling of being hurt and hit that Hemingway concentrates on, rather than alarming fears about its
long-term effects. In *For Whom the Bell Tolls* Robert
Jordan's injuries in themselves form a very small part of
the final dramatic scene of the novel. As for the "wounds"
that Nick Adams continues to get as a "growing boy,"
they are no more than setbacks any growing person
receives at the hands of life.

Thus, aside from *Across the River and Into the Trees,*
no other work of Hemingway projects the concept of the
wound so conspicuously. But here Hemingway seems to
be morbidly occupying himself with the worn-out body
of the old Colonel.

The Colonel arrives in Venice and on meeting the *Gran
Maestro,* a member of the Order of the Caballeros, he goes
over his memories of Grappa, Pasubio, and Basso Piave.
It is then that we learn that the "Supreme Commander,"
as the *Gran Maestro* calls the Colonel, has not only had
many concussions and small wounds and one really big
wound, but he also has a "crooked hand," deformed because of an injury.[10] The Colonel goes over to his room
in the hotel, and the waiter brings in a drink for him.
We now hear of the Colonel's ugliness ("Did you ever
see a more ugly face?") as though this were some sort of
additional injury. The Colonel then goes out to meet his
mistress, the Countess, and the ugly hand is brought forth
in another form. We see that Countess Renata is a fetish-

worshiper, and the hand for her has been serving as a sexual dream symbol.

"Let me feel your hand," she said. "It's all right. You can put it on the table."

"Thank you," the Colonel said.

"Please don't," she said. "I wanted to feel it because all last week, every night, or I think nearly every night, I dreamed about it and it was a strange mixed-up dream and I dreamed it was the hand of Our Lord."

"That's bad. You oughtn't to do that."

"I know it. That's just what I dreamed."

"You aren't on the junk, are you?"

"I don't know what you mean and please don't make fun when I tell you something true. I dreamed just as I say."

"What did the hand do?"

"Nothing. Or maybe that is not true. Mostly it was just a hand."

The Colonel here comes forward to help her out, and raises his hand straight up in front of her.

"Like this one?" The Colonel asked, looking at the mis-shapen hand with distaste and remembering the two times that had made it that way.

"Not like. It *was* that one. May I touch it carefully with my fingers if it does not hurt."[11]

There is an obsessive quality about the passage that cannot be ignored. (Hemingway uses the stump as sexual symbol in *To Have and Have Not* also, where in a sexual intercourse between Harry Morgan and Marie Morgan, Marie repeatedly urges her husband to place the stump on her body.) The Countess is only a young girl of nineteen, and there is absolutely no justification offered by

Hemingway for the deep passion that exists between her and the Colonel. E. M. Forster makes an important distinction between a story and a plot in his *Aspects of the Novel*. A story, he says, is a development which we are asked to accept *per se*. He offers a miniature, one-sentence novel as his illustration: The King died and the queen died. Fine, he says, this is quite a good story. But he argues that in order for the story to rise to the level of plot, we should not only have development but a justification for that development, too. The improved version of the one-sentence novel that he gives is: The King died and the queen died of grief. Now, he says, it is a perfect plot; we have the reason for the queen's death suitably explained for us.

Seen as such, *Across the River and Into the Trees* does not go beyond the level of commonplace storytelling. We can understand the love of Brett and Jake Barnes, of Catherine and Frederick Henry, or of Maria and Robert Jordan. There is, in each case, a fictional vindication of the growth and sequence of that love. But not so in the case of Renata and Colonel Cantwell.

Not only is there the barrier of age between them; from what we see of them in the novel, their tastes differ as well. Yet this girl is willing to submit herself completely to the Colonel. Even his ugliness seems to excite her sexually, and a measure of fetish worship cannot be discounted from her character. The sobriquet "Daughter" that Colonel Cantwell uses for her is again indicative of fetishism. The Colonel wants no love from her; he wants a daughter to care for his wounds!

And the wounds keep piling up. It is not clear whether the two times that the hand was hurt are included with the one major and many minor wounds mentioned earlier or are separate entries. But it does not hurt the Colonel there, he tells Renata soon afterwards. "Where it hurts is in the head, the legs and the feet."[12] So we have now two more deformed parts of the Colonel's body, the legs and the feet. But the story does not end here. We are further told that the Colonel also has a "broken nose,"[13] and that his whole face has in fact been subjected to elaborate plastic surgery:

> It looks as though it had been cut out of wood by an indifferent craftsman, he thought.
>
> He looked at the different welts and ridges that had come before they had plastic surgery, and at the thin, only to be observed by the initiate, lines of the excellent plastic operations after head wounds.[14]

Details about the hand are improved. The same evening Renata speaks about it once again. Having been out for a walk, they make a brief trip upstairs to the Colonel's room in the hotel (with nothing happening), and are now having dinner in the dining room below. "Please let me feel it," she says once again. And now we learn that the hand is split in the center. " 'Just be careful around the center,' the Colonel said. 'It's split there and it still cracks open.' "[15]

The Colonel wants to run his hand through Renata's hair, and Renata wants to be assured that it is the "hurt" hand that he would be doing it with.[16] Later in the night comes the love-making in the gondola and, to be sure, the subject of the hand crops up again. This time the Colonel prods her on, by asking, "Why do you like the hand?"[17] He now, however, places it where it belongs, that is on her body (as Harry Morgan does on his wife's in *To Have and Have Not*), and curiously enough, once that purpose has been served, the hand altogether disappears from the book (except for a brief reference to it in chapter 32).

Of course one wound is still there, for which the reckoning is yet to come: the heart, or "the main muscle," as Hemingway calls it. Of this I shall speak later. The important point is that in none of Hemingway's other novels is there such an unwholesome attachment to one fixed idea, the wounds of the body, as in *Across the River and Into the Trees*.

ii

This is not to say that there are not interesting things in the novel. On the contrary, the theme of death that Hemingway touched on in "The Snows of Kilimanjaro" and briefly also in *For Whom the Bell Tolls* is a touching one and Hemingway had an enormous opportunity of expanding it here. Yet, he misses that opportunity. In spite of this, there are occasional moments of extreme beauty in the story.

These are the moments when the narrative is at a stop, and the novelist is, in conformity with the structure he adopts in his other novels, introducing a diastolic pause. We have such pauses from the very beginning. The Colonel, the ugly, deformed Colonel, does have a private world of his own where he is inviolate. From time to time he lapses into that world, depending on the pressure of the moment. He knows he is going to die; in the duck-shooting scene with which the novel opens, he knows that every shot may well be his last and he does not want anything or anyone to ruin the sanctity of his private world. The boatman of the boat the Colonel is being rowed in is trying to break the ice around them for the boat to go through, and although the noise irritates the Colonel, his spontaneous response is "I do not understand him but I must not let him ruin it."[18] While being medically examined by his doctor, again what the Colonel wants is to finish with it and be on his own, with the quiet of his own self. "He was anxious for the interview to terminate. He was also anxious to lie down and take a seconal."[19]

So we see that there is a private world for the Colonel, which exists in spite of appearances to the contrary. It is the same world of which Hemingway's other major characters are conscious too—a world of greater realities, of greater complexities, which impinges on the life of man and, although it baffles and confuses him because it is so much wider and bigger than the small life of man that man cannot seem to contain it, it also allows man images of a wild beauty, a wild power, that surpasses everything he has ever known.

The Colonel, we observe, is acutely conscious of that larger world:

> Why should it always move your heart to see a sail moving along through the country, the Colonel thought. Why does it move my heart to see the great, slow, pale oxen? It must be the gait as well as the look of them and the size and the color.
>
> But a good fine big mule, or a string of pack mules in good condition, moves me, too. So does a coyote every time I ever see one, and a wolf, gaited like no other animal, gray and sure of himself, carrying that heavy head and with the hostile eyes.[20]

The Colonel, while traveling to Venice and thinking of these things, is deeply moved, and he tries to convey his awareness of the enormous many-sidedness of life to Jackson, the life which includes the helpful ox and the pack mule and the coyote and the wicked wolf all in the same common pack. But Jackson does not function at that level of awareness and remains unmoved. The Colonel, however,

> continued to look and it was all as wonderful to him and it moved him as it had when he was eighteen years old and had seen it first, understanding nothing of it and only knowing that it was beautiful.[21]

The phrase "understanding nothing of it and only knowing that it was beautiful" has an extreme relevance to the Hemingway world. The spontaneous response that comes involuntarily is the major concern of this novelist in his aesthetic representations.

After the Colonel has arrived in Venice, he meets with the *Gran Maestro* and there comes that great bluff about the Order to which they belong. Both treat the Order as a joke, but they appear to be quite attached to it as well, since the Order reminds them of their past. But this is how the Colonel spontaneously reacts when the diastolic pause comes along, after the *Gran Maestro* has left him alone: "Why am I always a bastard and why can I not suspend this trade of arms, and be a kind and good man as I would have wished to be."[22]

The systolic action and diastolic pauses run side by side, and the diastolic pauses give us a truer reflection of the Colonel. It is explained on the title page of *A Moveable Feast* that Hemingway used that phrase with reference to Paris in a letter to a friend in 1950: "If you are lucky enough to have lived in Paris as a young man, then wherever you go for the rest of your life, it stays with you, for Paris is a moveable feast." But it seems that, in reality, in that expression Hemingway was more concerned with the ultimate end of man, and with questions of ultimate pain and ultimate pleasure than with the pleasure he derived out of Paris or any other single association of life. For we see the same phrase used in *Across the River and Into the Trees* (a novel written at the same time as the letter to the friend about Paris, in 1950), and used in the general concept of man's happiness, man's end on this earth.

Arnaldo, the waiter, and Colonel Cantwell are talking in the latter's room in the hotel:

"Please call the desk and ask them to ring this number." The waiter made the call while the Colonel was in the bathroom.

"The Contessa is not at home, my Colonel," he said. "They believe you might find her at Harry's."

"You find everything on earth at Harry's."

"Yes, my Colonel. Except, possibly, happiness."

"I'll damn well find happiness, too," the Colonel assured him. "Happiness, as you know, is a movable feast."[23]

What apparently was uppermost in Hemingway's mind at this phase in his writing was the ultimate purpose of man's existence. As may be imagined, he transfers much of this concern to the character of the time, Colonel Cantwell. In the diastolic pauses in the story, the Colonel's semi-metaphysical concerns are all too prominent.

In other words, Hemingway in his later novels explicitly starts associating his characters with the extended world of total nature, and the essential fusion that the male character now desires is not so much with woman as with that other larger world. Symbolic of that wild communion is the sea and the big fish in *The Old Man and the Sea*; in *Across the River and Into the Trees*, it is the landscape and the canals and the gondola. The beauty of the landscape and the animal life that he sees and how these things move Colonel Cantwell has already been recorded, but we should also see the special attraction Colonel Cantwell feels for the gondola and the special relationship he comes to establish with it:

> They went out the side door of the hotel to the *imbarca-dero* and the wind hit them. The light from the hotel shone on the blackness of the gondola and made the water green. She looks as lovely as a good horse or as a racing shell, the Colonel thought. Why have I never seen a gondola before? What hand or eye framed that dark-ed symmetry?[24]

The last line seems an adaptation of the last line of Blake's poem "The Tiger." The Colonel is undoubtedly forming associations or fusions in his mind that go beyond the fusion with a human; the reference to the mysterious fountainhead of life is unmistakable. No wonder the love between Cantwell and Renata is consummated only in the physical domain of that new medium. No wonder Renata calls the gondola "our home."

> They got down into the gondola and there was the same magic, as always, of the light hull and the sudden displacement that you made and then the trimming in the dark privacy and then the second trimming, as the gondolier started to scull, laying her partly on her side so that he would have more control.[25]

iii

All these—Colonel Cantwell's concern for the larger life of the universe, his intuitive awareness of the beauty that surrounds him, the beauty of nature, and his periodical lapses into the diastolic mood—are present in *Across the River and Into the Trees*. But in spite of that, one cannot accept it as a great novel, because of the lack of inventiveness in the story. The genius of Hemingway that grasped the despair or glory of life in its relative context, that saw each aspect of life in its immediacy and then sublimated it in the ultimate force of total life fails him at this juncture.

Hemingway's heroes are praised by me essentially for their sensitivity, for the absence of the demanding ego—for their passivity. Nothing in the entire *Across the River and Into the Trees* more demonstrates the temporary suspension or absence of the creative faculty than the relative insensitivity that comes to occupy the protagonist, Colonel Cantwell.

In comparison with Hemingway's other heroes, Colonel Cantwell is a self-centered egoist. It is difficult to determine whether he is so by temperament or whether it is age that has done this to him. Considering the sensitivity he shows while in tune with nature, one would ascribe his egoism to old age. But he seems to be in constant need of self-assertion as a preliminary to self-assurance. Even at a time when Renata asks him where he should like to be buried after his death, he has to remind himself of his "victories" when he gives the answer to her—"On any part of the high ground where we beat them."[26] The long account that he gives to Renata of the Allied victory in Europe in the second world war, an account extending over five or six chapters, smacks of an urgent desire to enlarge his own image of himself. At the same time, he is bitter too. "I'll tell you how it was . . . and General Walter Bedell Smith doesn't know how it was yet. Though, probably, I am wrong, as I have been so many times."[27] The bitterness persists, but then one realizes that he rather welcomes that bitterness and nurses it. "How can I remember if I am not bitter?"[28] he tells himself reassuringly. When Renata questions him, "But are you bitter about everything?" again the conceited reply is, "No. It is just that I am half a hundred years old and I know things."[29]

If Hemingway had held his grasp on his creative method, he would have shown the conceit of Colonel Cantwell as part of the life story of a man who was a *failure*. It is as a "failed" Colonel alone that the character of Colonel Cantwell can be justified and upheld at the fictional level. As a failed Colonel, his ego, his need for self-assertion, his necessity to justify himself, can be understood and accepted. In brief snatches, he is passive enough to indulge in the luxury of self-criticism:

> What miserable career did you attempt and have failed at?
>
> I wished to be, and was, a General Officer in the Army of the United States. I have failed and I speak badly of all who have succeeded.[30]

But such passages are rare in the novel, and they come in a mocking tone, which suggests that the Colonel does not quite believe in what he is saying—that he is uttering these words as though they were the criticism made of him by someone else, with which criticism he himself did not agree. For the dominant note of his statements is one of self-glorification. With Jackson, with the *Gran Maestro,* with Renata, the image is that of a victorious hero. It is for this reason that one finds it hard to accept his bitterness.

Also, at no level is the bitterness surmounted or sublimated. In the other novels, the hero invariably manages to rise above the bitter mood of the moment, or at least remains conscious of the "smallness" of his bitterness. Not so Colonel Cantwell.

That Colonel Cantwell can be strikingly insensitive can be further seen from the way he discourses on the subject of killing. In *For Whom the Bell Tolls* the same subject—the killing of man by man—is brought up several times and Robert Jordan and Anselmo both show an aversion to it. But Colonel Cantwell takes pride in being a professional killer; he calls it his "trade."[31] Not only that. He keeps a full list of the number that have died at his hand and has no regrets while reporting on the matter.

Renata and Colonel Cantwell are speaking:

"How many have you killed?"
"One hundred and twenty-two sures. Not counting possibles."
"You had no remorse?"
"Never."
"Nor bad dreams about it?"
"Nor bad dreams. But usually strange ones. Combat dreams, always, for a while after combat. But then strange dreams about places mostly. We live by accidents of terrain, you know. And terrain is what remains in the dreaming part of your mind."[32]

The worst thing one notices in Colonel Cantwell, and by extension in the novel itself, is that the periods of diastolic pause are not so creative and productive for the Colonel as they are for the other heroes. Not that Hemingway changes the structure. The structure remains the same; after a stretch of systolic activity, the diastolic pause emerges in the fiction. But Colonel Cantwell is out of tune, and he is only partially sensitive to such moments. For the sake of illustration, let us take the five chapters, chapters 15 through 19, when the Colonel is alone in his room, and when there is a diastolic pause in the narrative. What has happened in the systolic action that precedes this pause is that Renata has presented the Colonel with a portrait of herself. That portrait is now there in the room, and the Colonel is looking at it. What follows in the five chapters is a recapitulation of what has gone before; the tone, the memories do not usher in anything new. Jake Barnes, Frederick Henry and Robert Jordan were totally altered in such pauses; their consciousness received a shock of renewal, and they afterwards admitted to having been changed. But the Colonel goes on in the diastolic mood almost untouched by it. "Here's to you, Daughter . . . You beauty and lovely. Do you know, that, among other things, you smell good always? You smell wonderfully even in a high wind or under a blanket or kissing good night. You know almost no one does, and you don't use scent."[33] This passage, which the Colonel addresses to the portrait, and which is typical of the tone and language of what follows in these five chapters, offers in no way a departure from the old. It is the same Colonel, using the same metaphors, and he emerges out of this diastolic pause very much the same type of man.

The other long diastolic pause in the novel, where the Contessa is sleeping with the Colonel in his room (chapters 34 and 35), offers no better moments of revelation and enlightenment. What the Colonel thinks at one stage is perhaps descriptive of the entire book. We read: "The Colonel and the girl lay quietly on the bed and the Colonel tried to think of nothing; as he had thought of nothing so many times in so many places. But it was no good now. It would not work any more because it was too late."[34]

In the present book, we have tried to associate the nothingness of which the Colonel is speaking with the

dark mysterious nothingness of larger life, the diastolic
rhythm of the universe, of which Hemingway makes one
sharply aware. That magic charm has vanished, not only
from Colonel Cantwell but from Hemingway also—at
least for the time being. It is as though Hemingway were
passing through a period of menopause, a change of life,
and did not quite know how best to adjust himself to
the altered rhythm which age brought along with it.
Across the River and Into the Trees is the product of
that period of menopause (if there could be a menopause
among men). It lacks the spontaneous joy with which his
other works are filled, and it has very little of inventiveness to it. There are many things "said" in the book. But
very little is "made up."

7

The Old Man and the Sea

In the letter that Hemingway sent to his publisher along with the manuscript of *The Old Man and the Sea*, he made the claim that this was the "best" that he had done in the course of a lifetime of learning to write, and that the novel could well stand as an "epilogue" to all his other works.[1] Coming from an artist who was most diffident in talking about his writings, it is an amazing statement of confidence not only in the virtue of the novel, but in his own method or technique. It also points to the unusual difficulties and complexities that Hemingway must have tried to resolve in this book.

The variety of response that *The Old Man and the Sea* has excited since its publication seems to be a testimony to the complex nature of the novel. The opinion of critics has alternated between extreme praise and extreme scepticism. The recently published volume of essays on the novel, in the Twentieth Century Interpretation series, gives some idea of the gulf that separates one group from the other.

It will serve no useful purpose to give an account of all those critical essays here. But before we go on, we should look briefly at some of them.

Robert P. Week in "Fakery in *The Old Man and the Sea*" takes exception to the "inexactness" he observes in *The Old Man and the Sea*. The old man Santiago, he

170

believes, is too strong physically, his fishing skill bordering on "clairvoyance," his marlin too heavy to be handled
by a single individual; and so on. Inexactness can be
traced in any writer, if that be the only purpose of our
reading his text. But Week's point is that Hemingway
introduced these inexactnesses on purpose to romanticize
the tale; that he was, in other words, a bluffer. This is
a harsh judgment on any creative writer. It is not the
purpose of a writer to produce an exact transcript of life.
His job is to evoke images with a view to producing a
sense of beauty. And then, how can anyone presuppose
that there *cannot* be a man like Santiago or a fish like
the marlin in *The Old Man and the Sea?* The writer
searches in a work for the ideal, in the hope that the ideal
somewhere exists. And even Hemingway's adverse critics
(Dwight Macdonald, Philip Toynbee, Cyril Connolly)
grant that he was a very "sincere" writer. "He was hope-
lessly sincere. His life, his writing, his public personality
and his private thoughts were all of a piece,"[3] said Dwight
Macdonald in an article in *Encounter*.

The editor of these essays, Katharine T. Jobes, observes
in her perceptive introduction: "The disagreement
[among critics] comes in evaluation rather than explica-
tion."[4] However, in that disagreement, there is a certain
unanimity which is interesting. It lies in the fact that
almost all these interpretations of the novel discuss the
story as an allegory on an either/or basis. That is, they
all see it as two forces pitched against each other. One
critic would say it is man against nature. Another, it is
the temporal against the eternal. Still another, old age
against youth. Another still, heresy against the Christian
faith. Thus the divergent interpretations are identical in
one respect: they oppose one set of values to another, and
see the whole novel as a "fight" between these two sets of

values or forces. Many critics have traced this novel to Hemingway's early story "The Undefeated" (and even those who do not approve of the novel as a great work, like Dwight Macdonald, approve of the short story), yet another indication of the "fight" that underlies the myth.

My own stand on the novel, as indeed on the rest of Hemingway, is that the work is not a presentation of contention or fight. I have suggested throughout that for Hemingway life existed in plurality and that there was no apparent contradiction for him in that plurality. There is the small life of the individual or any other living creature; and then there is the total life of the universe, which includes and transcends the smaller life of any one particular living organism. The individual no doubt has to pursue his life at his own level. But from time to time he becomes strangely aware of the other, larger life. But there is no inherent "fight" in that awareness. Such moments are rather moments of revelation for him, and come to him when he is in a passive mood. He then goes on with his life in a greater awareness of the total meaning of being alive.

But a part of Hemingway always remained resentful of this vision. Hemingway's intelligence as an artist made him see clearly that the plural nature of the universe could alone explain the life and death cycle to which each living organism is subject. But as a man Hemingway also felt hurt at this vision, for it did not give man the supreme position in the scheme of the universe. What happens in *The Old Man and the Sea* is that Hemingway's resentment against this vision altogether vanishes. Various forms of life are mentioned here, where each form preys on the other for food and life and then in turn becomes a prey to another so that that other life may go on—a vision close enough to and probably derived from Blake's *Marriage of Heaven and Hell.* And in this enormous drama of life, there is no resentment felt by one kind of life against another, nor is there any resentment or bitterness on the part of the novelist who is portraying the play of life for us.

The story thus presents a unique theme—the theme of resignation. Santiago is not pitched in battle against anything in the story; there is no either/or survival fight. Consequently there is no victory for man, as most readings of the novel have tried to establish. That this is being said, that the concept of victory is being rejected, does not imply that the contrary concept of "defeat" is being promoted. Such divisive or contradictory terms or ways of thinking split up the beauty of Hemingway's unified vision. If there is no victory for Santiago, moral or physical, there is no defeat either. Santiago neither wins nor loses; he is just resigned to what ultimately does happen to him. He is the purest and the most passive of Hemingway's passive heroes.

That the theme of *The Old Man and the Sea* is resignation, we can understand better if we deal a little more elaborately with the either/or myth. The most obvious of these either/or juxtapositions is man against fate. But in the novel there is no hostile destiny or fate that man has to fight all the time; fate as an abstract power pitched against man (as in the novels of Thomas Hardy) does not figure here. The same fate that has not given Santiago a fish for eighty-four days has given many to other fishermen; on the very three days that Santiago is wrestling with the marlin, Manolin catches "one the first day. One the second and two the third."[5] Then the same Santiago who is now so unlucky was not always unlucky. His skill in fishing, to which endless references are made, and the accounts he gives of the big fishing done by him earlier, are suggestive of great successes. Like everyone else, he has been lucky on occasions; on other occasions, like the present one, he has been unlucky. In any given moment, fate is kind to some, unkind to others.

Hence, it is not a malicious fate that functions in Hemingway. What is conceived is a power bigger than man, which works according to a set of secret permutations. On the whole it is a benign force, as in one's immediate life it bestows on man many benedictions. But if one tempts it too much, if one asks too much of it, he must be prepared for disappointments. This is what Santiago means when, at the end of the novel, he repeatedly says: "I went too far out."[6] It is not an accusation of a power which is only over there in the "out" and not here in our immediate neighbourhood, as some critics have asserted. For one thing, the old man did not go too far out by choice, he was dragged there by the fish. Secondly, the old man is not for a second afraid of the sea or of a power that may be there too far out. He calls the sea *la mar*—"as feminine and as something that gave or withheld great favours, and if she did wild or wicked things it was because she could not help them."[7] The question of distance does not come into this concept; the sea could be as wicked a foot away from the shore as too far out. Also, the same man who says "I went too far out," has this to say about the distance business: "no man was ever alone on the sea,"[8] and "a man is never lost at sea and it is a long island."[9]

So what Santiago means by "I went too far out" (a statement that has been quoted by critics to justify the either/or myth), is that he took too big a risk and hence multiplied his chances of failure. He could have come back successful even from a long trip, to be sure;

failure is not implicit in the distance. As it happens, he is coming back as a failure.

Similarly, too much is made of the old man versus the boy allegory. It is true that the old man constantly thinks of the boy while fishing, and he wishes that the boy were there with him: "I wish the boy was here," and "I wish I had the boy." But there is nothing in the story to indicate that the old man resents his age or that these phrases represent a nostalgic longing for his youth. Colonel Cantwell in *Across the River and Into the Trees* resents his age; but not Santiago. He, rather, is vain about his age, for age has taught him tricks which the young do not know. Like the ancient mariner, he thinks of himself as "a strange old man," who has a measure of unbeatable power in him. As he says to the boy: "I may not be as strong as I think, but I know many tricks and I have resolution."[10] Again and again he asserts: "There are plenty of things I can do." And the boy, in the end, tells him the same. He wants to return to the old man, luck or no luck, "for I still have much to learn," and again, "You must get well fast for there is much that I can learn and you can teach me everything."[11]

It is difficult in the face of this evidence to read the novel as an allegory of old age longing for the return of youth. The old man can do without the boy; it is the boy who cannot do without the old man. He is unhappy with the other man, who does not treat him as an equal and will not even let him carry his boat gear. But the old man says to the boy: "I let you carry things when you were five years old."[12] Santiago recalls the memory of the boy very simply because the presence of the boy would be of use to him as additional help. Moreover, the boy was with the old man for the first forty days of the present run of bad luck, and it would be only natural for the old man to think of him out of habit.

Likewise, the view of the novel as a Christian allegory, deriving its symbols partly from Christianity, cannot be sustained upon a close analysis of the text. "Just as the great marlin in his noble but futile struggle to preserve his life becomes identified symbolically with the crucified Christ, so the old man in his noble but futile struggle to preserve the fish from the sharks becomes identified with the same figure."[13] So writes Arvin R. Wells in "A Ritual of Transfiguration: The *Old Man and the Sea*." Wells does not notice that the story in general revolves more around pagan myths than Christian ones. For the cosmos of *The Old Man and the Sea* is a self-perpetuating cosmos, complete in itself, running on an elaborate system of mutations and internal rhythms and needing no external divinity to shape its course. The old man does refer to his hands once as though a nail were driven through them. But to conclude on the basis of that that he is a Christ symbol would be farfetched. Worse still would be to identify Santiago with the Cain figure, as Wells at one stage does, since the old man kills his brother, the fish. If we think of him as Cain, perforce we will have to think of him as Abel too, for every organism in the novel is a dual entity: it kills others for food, and itself perishes in course of time to provide food for others.

Wells declares that at the end Santiago has won his "freedom to dream uninterruptedly of the lions,"[14] since previously the old man was always called back to further action and further suffering. And what has happened now? Has that necessity been satisfied? Must not the old man get up the very next day and go out fishing again? Must he not eat? Wherein lies the peace? The peace of exhaustion—the nullity of exhaustion, rather—should not be confused with the peace of fulfillment. So far as the last sleep is concerned, it marks only the completion of a cycle. The story is brought to the same point where it was at the opening. Again the old man is without a fish for many days. Again there is the boy beside him. Again the old man is sure and confident of himself. The clue to the aesthetic purpose of the story, on the contrary, lies in the attitude that Santiago displays all along.

ii

It is in Santiago's attitude of resignation that *The Old Man and the Sea* acquires a tremendous magnitude. Santiago is not busy in a fight with nature; he is living his life in terms of acceptance (of things over which he has little control). Not for a moment does it enter the old man's head that he is in any way superior to the rest of life around him; he does not consider himself superior to the fish he has hooked, either. "Man is not much beside the great birds and beasts,"[15] says the old man. And whenever he does speak of his superiority to the fish, he does so disparagingly—"I am only better than him through trickery,"[16] or "I was only better armed."[17] Throughout the story he calls the fish his "brother," as indeed he calls every other created organism. It is as a part of that vast cosmic drama that the old man takes note of himself; never in pride, only in humility. And it is in that humility that the true glory of the old man lies.

The pain that the old man suffers in the story is not his personal pain; it is rather the pain of the process of being alive. For Hemingway, this pain has been the theme of his entire work. The larger life of the universe is flamboyant and all-powerful. In that larger life, the individual has his own smaller life, which smaller life is itself in some measure an expression of the power and beauty of the larger life of the universe. But in the context of that larger life, the small life of the individual must perforce one day end and is therefore by implication tragic in its scope; hence the pain of that awareness.

The limited pursuit of the old man is the hunt of the fish. Without that he can make no living and would soon starve to death. In that pursuit the old man is shown in absolute mastery of his trade. He is skillful, he keeps his material in readiness, his fishing lines are "straighter" than those of any other fisherman, and most of all he is "exact."[18] He knows the direction of the wind; when he is in a sea current he intuitively "feels" the touch of it on his skiff; he can read his position from the stars; he is "a strange old man" who, in his own words, knows "many tricks,"[19] and the boy Manolin is indeed right when he tells him that he has a uniqueness about him unequaled by any fisherman: "There are many good fishermen and some great ones. But there is only you!"[20]

The very physical personality of the old man makes him out to be a uniquely powerful figure and lends him a symbolic grandeur:

> The old man was thin and gaunt with deep wrinkles in the back of his neck. The brown blotches of the benevolent skin cancer the sun brings from its reflection on the tropic sea were on his cheeks. The blotches ran well down the sides of his face and his hands had the deep-creased scars from handling heavy fish on the cords. But none of these scars were fresh. They were as old as erosions in a fishless desert.[21]

Comparisons between *The Old Man and the Sea* and *The Ancient Mariner* have occasionally been made, but it must be seen that there is nothing metaphysical or mysterious about the old man. Nor does Hemingway (unlike Coleridge) bring in the supernatural machinery to create the atmosphere of the tale. The ancient mariner was at the mercy of, indeed was a tool of supernatural forces. The old man, even in his worst moments, never loses his head. He owes his strength to no one but himself.

Now if there is any "victory" at all for the old man in the novel, it is a victory in the context of the smaller life of the man. The old man cannot bring the fish home, but there is no question that he returns a victor. He may have lost the fish to the sharks, but that is not owing to lack of courage or skill on his part. He gives up only when it is too dark, and when he is left with nothing to carry on the fight; the harpoon, the gaff, the rudder, the oar with the blade are all gone. In the fight with the fish the old man is undoubtedly the winner. But then it is a victory which was never in dispute. The way Hemingway projects the figure of the old man, it was inevitable that he should win against the fish.

However, in the larger life of the universe, the old man definitely suffers a defeat. " 'They beat me, Manolin. They truly beat me.' "[22] The "they" of the sentence is the plurality of life that surrounds the old man—the plurality that includes the old man, but also includes the gulf weed, the shrimp, the man-of-war bird, the delicate tern, the schools of bonito and albacore, the tuna and the flying fish, the dolphin, the turtle, the plankton, the warbler, the big marlin, and all the sharks.

It must be repeated that it is not suggested here that the larger life of the universe pursues man with malice or vengeance and imposes a defeat on him in every single encounter. Once the old man had been without a fish for eighty-seven days, but then he caught "big ones every day for three weeks."[23] What is suggested is that these two lives—of the individual and of the universe—run simultaneously, and the individual must be prepared to yield the right of way.

That is precisely what the old man has learned to do in his life—to accept defeat at the hands of the larger life of the universe gracefully and with resignation, and Hemingway in the novel presents a masterly fusion of the two lives or the two modes of living. The old man is conscious of his own power and ability, but he is also conscious of the power and glory of the universe. In resigning himself to the larger life of the universe, the old man does not lose in stature; rather, he rises above the limitations of the smaller life of the individual and acquires heroic proportions. The old man is the most passive of Hemingway's heroes not in the absence of physical power in him or in the will to work. It is because he alone of all his heroes accepts the larger life of the universe without bitterness. He is all-powerful, but he is also all-humble.

It is on this note of humility that the hunt of the great fish begins. For eighty-four days the old man has been without a fish, and with courage and determination he is getting ready to go out once again. The boy cannot go with him—his parents have taken him away from him, regarding the old man as unlucky. But the boy offers the old man a beer, and the old man modestly accepts it. The boy then offers to get fresh sardines for him, to bait the fish with, and also a few baits. Again the old man modestly accepts the offer. And we have these words from Hemingway which go with this moment, describing the mental state of the old man. "He was too simple to wonder when he had attained humility. But he knew he had attained it and he knew it was not disgraceful and it carried no loss of true pride."[24]

Ensues a vast drama on land and the sea, and involving

the various creatures that live in the sea. The old man is only an illiterate fisherman, and his awareness of the larger life of the universe has not come to him through knowledge or self-analysis. It has come to him through his passivity, through his humility. As he rows out into the sea, he intuitively thinks in terms of the plurality of things. He knows for certain that the sea "is kind and very beautiful."[25] But he also knows that she can be "so cruel."[26] The sea is also a beloved—"the moon affects her as it does a woman."[27] In this sea live the mighty fish. But there also fly birds that are "so delicate and fine."[28]

In the three-day sojourn on the sea, the total image that is projected by Hemingway is an image of fusion. Everything is mutated against something else, and exists in relation to the rest of the life. Even the bait hanging down into the water is projected as an image of that fusion. The old man sits in his boat, holding the bait. At the other end of the bait are the hooks and the sardines. "Each bait hung head down with the shank of the hook inside the bait fish, tied and sewed solid and all the projecting part of the hook, the curve and the point, was covered with fresh sardines. Each sardine was hooked through both eyes so that they made a half-garland on the projecting steel."[29] Later, when the old man has the big fish at the other end and cannot yet kill it, he is not sure who is fishing for whom. The only certainty is that they are hooked to each other and there is a fusion. (The stage for this was prepared by Hemingway much in advance. Even while the old man is waiting for the fish with his baits down, it looks as though the fish were circling around him to get *him*.)

There are innumerable other images of fusion scattered through the story; fusion symbolic of plurality and yet of the oneness that runs through plurality. Very early we see the ritualistic fusion of the old man with the boy. A man-of-war bird is shown flying over a dolphin and the flying fish, and together they somehow form a common axis. Then a relationship between the turtles, whose hearts continue to beat even when they are cut up and butchered, and the old man is established. The old man not only eats turtle eggs to make himself strong, but he feels toward the turtles that "I have such a heart too and my feet and hands are like theirs."[30] Follows the tragic tale of the two marlin, one male and one female, when the old man hooked the female and the male kept circling around, until he came out wide-eyed to see where the female was lying in the boat. They remain indivisible even in death, and the mystery of it to the old man lay in the fact that the male had not gone away, and though only fish, he had the capacity and courage to stay with his mate. "He was beautiful, the old man remembered, and he had stayed."[31] Finally there is the great fusion between the old man and the big fish, which is projected through many angles—of physical pain, of hunger, of fear.

And throughout, the old man is completely resigned to the comparative freedom that each living organism has to act, including man. There are absolutely no expressions of *nada* in *The Old Man and the Sea*. There is no bitterness, no denial; there is only acceptance.

The courage that the old man displays is not a defiance of fate or destiny; rather, it is an assertion of the obligation that each man has to himself—it is more an act of duty. When the old man declares, "But man is not made for defeat . . . A man can be destroyed but not defeated,"[32] he is not defying his fate. What he means by this is that a man has an obligation to himself to go on in spite of the defeat. He knows very well that a man *can* be defeated, for he has just been defeated himself and he later admits it to the boy ("They beat me, Manolin. They truly beat me"). But the sentence, "A man can be destroyed but not defeated," is a remarkable expression of the faith of the old man (and of Hemingway) in the dignity of man. What the old man means is that a man can never be defeated out of his will to go on—until he falls. The stress is on dignity, even when the odds are against one. "Take a good rest, small bird . . . Then go in and take your chance like any man or bird or fish."[33]

The old man is thus utterly reconciled to his destiny and is not only the most passive of Hemingway's heroes, he is the noblest. In the presentation of the story of the old man, Hemingway is able to offer a unified view of the plurality of life that had escaped him earlier.

iii

In terms of the structure of the novel, the systolic and the diastolic moods are so clearly alternated in *The Old Man and the Sea* that any reader of the novel should be able to locate them without much effort. The old man and his life are like the colossal heartbeat of the entire universe. The old man wakes up, the old man sleeps. The old man works, the old man rests. The old man draws in the line, the old man plays it out. The old man eats, the old man stands up to urinate, to pass out waste. The old man is without luck for many days, but then he is lucky for weeks running. In sleep itself, the old man dreams and then again he sleeps without dreams.

The entire novel runs on this diurnal rhythm of activity and repose. The systolic parts of the action are where the old man is busy catching the fish. The diastolic parts are where he is trying to come to terms with his destiny as a man. But the two modes come one after the other, and neither is absent for too long.

The preparations for the eighty-fifth day of the hunt begin on a systolic note, with the conversation between the old man and the boy. That's how the novel opens. But as soon as the boy goes off to get the sardines, the old man drifts into a private world of his own—he goes to sleep. In order to accentuate the diastolic rhythm of the larger life into which for the moment he has lapsed, Hemingway for a while tells us nothing about the fish or about the old man's worries. Instead, the images in the paragraph where we find the old man sleeping identify him with the eternal and not with the temporal; they identify him with the limitless, abstract forces of the larger life that will never pass away. His head we read is "old" and his shoulders "powerful" and "strange" and his patched-up shirt looks like a "sail"—all suggestive not so much of his present misery but of the endurance of man through the ages. For the time being the old man ceases to be an old fisherman; he becomes an old everyman.

The alternate rhythm between the systolic and the diastolic modes now continues. The boy returns and wakes him up and gives him his supper (systolic). Again the old man goes to sleep and there is peace for him (diastolic). The next morning the old man departs for the sea, throws out his baits, and is ready for the fish (systolic). He then lapses into a rhapsody about the turtles and his affinity with them (diastolic). The old man tries to fish by following the movements of a bird and catches an albacore (systolic). The old man indulges in the luxury of talking to himself—"he did not remember when he had first started to talk aloud when he was by himself"[34] (diastolic).

At this point in the story, the old man is in a blissful diastolic mood: "I could just drift, he thought, and sleep and put a bight of line around my toe to wake me. But today is eighty-five days and I should fish the day well."[35]

So he has to go on and return to the systolic mode, and it is precisely at this time that the big fish takes a bite of the hook and starts pulling the old man away from land to the northwest (systolic). Follows the night, and through that night no systolic action takes place; the old man passively listens to the sound of two porpoises that have come along and are rolling by the side of the boat, and he thinks of the time that he had hooked a female marlin and the male had refused to leave his beloved (diastolic). During the day a bird comes along and the old man is willing to offer it hospitality (systolic). But then the sight of the helpless bird in that wide and wild sea sets the old man pitying the bird for its fate, and without even being aware of it he lapses into the diastolic mood. He is shaken out of this mood rudely when the fish gives a pull and the old man's hand starts bleeding (systolic). "How did I let the fish cut me with that one quick pull he made? I must be getting very stupid. Or perhaps I was looking at the small bird and thinking of him."[36]

This is the pattern that continues all along. The old man sees the fish for the first time now, when it rises out of the sea and falls back into it. Eventually in the fight that is magnificently portrayed, the fish is killed by the old man on the third day after it first got hooked (systolic). Immediately the old man is sorry for the fish and the other mode returns—"I have killed this fish . . .

my brother"[37] (diastolic). In the long journey back home, the old man is attacked by the sharks and again the old man fights back courageously and Hemingway captures that fight for us with much power and immediacy (systolic). But alongside, there is another feeling in the old man's heart, the passive feeling that he had taken too big a risk by going so far out and should now be prepared for the consequences—"It was too good to last, he thought"[38] (diastolic).

It should be observed that there is no regret in the old man for killing the fish; at no stage does Hemingway soil the purity of his passive awareness through ethical generalizations. The old man is not feeling remorseful after the sharks have taken away his catch, or feeling guilty. He is only sorry for the chance's turning against him, which chance could as well have turned in his favor.

The old man returns to his port, goes to his shack and falls asleep, where the boy discovers him the next morning. Again the old man is not remorseful, nor has he given up. He has done his duty, but he has to go on. For we have seen earlier that the old man looks at the experience of each day as the start of a new adventure: "Each time was a new time and he never thought about the past when he was doing it."[39]

The theme of resignation acquires a more pointed meaning when seen through the recurring pattern in which the narrative is presented to us. While the old man is ever willing for action, he is also ever willing to submit to the larger forces of life that surround him.

Much is made by some critics of the meaning of the old man's dreams—the actual dreams and his daydreams, dreams of DiMaggio and the African sea beaches and the lions. The thing to be observed first is the bringing in by Hemingway of the sleep or dream sequences into the fabric of the novel. If it is a novel of action, what are these dreams doing here? By introducing the dream sequences into the story, Hemingway introduces another rhythm into it. They are suggestive of the inner repose of the old man; they are suggestive of peace, of diastolic peace. For we see that the old man's dreams are dreams of a harmony unique in itself. "He no longer dreamed of storms, nor of women, nor of great occurrences, nor of great fish, nor fights, nor contests of strength, nor of his wife."[40] He does not even dream about "the boy." The idea is that every image suggestive of contention has vanished from his consciousness. What he dreams of now is only "places" or he dreams of "the lions on the beach."

The lions and DiMaggio are simply perfection symbols, which supplement the old man's awareness of that larger universe. The lion we know is the king of the beasts—*El Campeón*. Similarly DiMaggio for the old man is "the great DiMaggio," a champion. And that is precisely what the old man himself was at one time and would still regard himself to be—Santiago *El Campeón*, as in the episode of his first match with the Negro.

When the old man thinks of DiMaggio or dreams of the lions, he identifies himself with things that are powerful in spite of the limitations of the world. He is an old man now, no longer as strong and young. But he knows that he has a power that still relates him to the universe. That is what his dreams imply—a center of stillness for his soul in the larger sea of the total life.

iv

In *The Old Man and the Sea* Hemingway reaches a measure of sanity, a sense of the fusion of the individual with the cosmos, that had eluded him earlier. As such,

The Old Man and the Sea must be recognized as his most successful novel, a point of culmination in his growth as an artist. That was the quest which his writer-character Harry had in mind when in "The Snows of Kilimanjaro" he speaks nostalgically of the pure experience that he wanted to convey and how he had frittered away his energies in other directions.

In a long passage in *Green Hills of Africa*, Hemingway offers a pertinent fusion of the temporal with the eternal, and shows how it was the business of the artist to capture the immortal beauty of that fusion.

> If you serve time for society, democracy, and the other things quite young, and declining any further enlistment make yourself responsible only to yourself, you exchange the pleasant, comforting stench of comrades for something you can never feel in any other way than by yourself.[41]

The passage begins with an assertion of the loneliness of the artist, or the lonely road that he must travel to arrive at that something special. Hemingway candidly admits that he cannot yet "completely define" what that something is, but then offers the suggestion that it is close to the feeling that comes "when you write well and truly of something and know impersonally that you have written it that way."[42] Other people may not recognize its merit; to begin with, they may even accuse the writer of being a "fake." But an artist, once he has accomplished writing of that quality, "know[s] its value absolutely."[43]

Hemingway then goes on to elaborate his image of that fusion of the individual with the eternal. He speaks of the Gulf Stream and its capacity to absorb the history of man into its flow. The stream has been flowing for centuries. For centuries, it has watched and taken into itself "the palm fronds of our victories, the worn light bulbs of our discoveries and the empty condoms of our great loves."[44] Men come and go, but the stream is still there. However, those men who live to the fullness of their power as individuals have a permanent place in the universe, since the stream of which they once partook will always flow and carry a part of their power in it: "Those that have always lived in it are permanent and of value because that stream will flow, as it has flowed."[45]

Hemingway's different novels were a quest of the artist in him for perfection, and in *The Old Man and the Sea* he reaches his aesthetic consummation. The book may truly be accepted as the epitaph to his entire career as a writer.

8

Conclusion

Hemingway was a poor aesthete, and was never able to formulate his creative theories into an essay or a long piece of sustained prose. Maybe it was a question of time. He wrote to Wallace Meyer in the office of Scribner's in 1952 that he did not have the leisure even to frame a letter properly; his best time and talent were reserved for creative writing.[1] But if we examine his life, particularly the early years when he learned to write, we notice how all his preoccupations were in fact with the craft of writing. So far as the themes of his works were concerned, he picked up what was most easily or readily available. If there was a war going on, he wrote on the war. If someone put it into his head that he and his contemporaries were a "lost generation," he wrote on the so-called lost generation. If there came about a civil war in a certain country, he wrote on the civil war. After the second world war, he set about to write a novel on that. When no other subject was available, he wrote on the Gulf Stream and the fishing that went on it. Or he wrote on his travels, on fishing trips in Michigan, or on scenes of domesticity, of domestic tension and domestic love.

It might appear strange, but Hemingway was not deeply involved with any one subject or any one special theme in his life. If we read his enormous correspondence with people, we see that most of those letters are what we would call business letters, about the sale of books, royalties, and stuff like that (to Maxwell Perkins, Scott Fitzgerald, etc.) and purely personal letters (to Major General Lanham, Janet Flanner, etc.). Nowhere in him does one see a passionate identification with any of the contemporary problems nor does he seem to have a cause to promote. If he wrote on the "lost generation" or on the Spanish war and fascism, it was not out of feelings of conviction; it was more a matter of expediency. Nor does one find in him any serious concern (at least not a concern which is articulated) for some of the abstract things of life, like the purpose of being alive, the future of man, or that flimsy thing called the human soul. Compared with the letters of a man like Lawrence or Keats, Hemingway's letters make poor reading indeed.

To generalize in this fashion is not to suggest that Hemingway's life or fiction preclude an appreciation of the graver things of life. As has been established here, his work springs from and revolves around an intense moral awareness of life, an intense moral seriousness. But Hemingway did not plan out his fiction to promote or solve any such problems. Only for a very short period, when he was writing *For Whom the Bell Tolls,* did he allow his name to be associated with a topical subject. Otherwise, as Edmund Wilson correctly stated in his review of Hemingway's first two thin books in the *Dial,* he was "not even a propagandist for humanity."[2] Hemingway went to the extent of writing to Miss Janet Flanner in 1933 that even when his memoirs were published—works which normally tend to be polemical—he would not go out of his way to prove any bloody thing (as he put it) there.[3] Somehow he conspicuously stayed aloof from issues and dogmas.

But structural and other artistic concerns claimed Hemingway's interest almost as pointedly as the interest in subjects and issues is absent. Though he did not formulate his aesthetic theories, he very definitely developed such theories and repeatedly tried them out to see how well they worked. All his energies were directed at his art rather than the content of his art.

ii

In this, Hemingway was singularly lucky in the crowd he moved with and the friends he picked up in Paris during the twenties. In Fenton's *The Apprenticeship of Ernest Hemingway*, the impression is given that Hemingway learned to write the way he did in his early years at the *Kansas City Star*, or the *Toronto Star*. His association as a journalist with these and other newspapers would certainly have helped him with his clipped, sinewy style. But his work as a journalist did not develop his talent as a creative writer, and his formative period as a writer begins not in Kansas City but only in Paris when he had gone back there with his wife in 1921.

A good part of his early years in Paris was spent rather in unlearning what he had learned as a journalist. In the introductory chapter of this book, reference is made to Hemingway's distinction between "reporting" a thing and "making up" a thing.

> In writing for a newspaper you told what happened and, with one trick and another, you communicated the emotion aided by the element of timeliness which gives a certain emotion to any account of something that has happened on that day; but the real thing, the sequence of motion and fact which made the emotion and which would be as valid in a year or in ten years or, with luck and if you

stated it purely enough, always, was beyond me and I was working very hard to try to get it.[4]

In the *Esquire* article in 1935, "Monologue to the Maestro: A High Seas Letter," the young man who wants to learn how to write asks Hemingway the same question: where will "good writing" differ from "reporting?" Hemingway, disguised as "Your Correspondent" in the article, gives the same reply: "It is made; not described."[5]

Thus, Hemingway was somewhat painfully conscious of the difference between the two forms of writing. He could describe an event or an emotion at the journalistic level. But to get to the real thing he had to learn to invent things, to make them up. Too much identification with one's subject, basing what one writes exactly on how one saw it in real life, was not an asset but a handicap. That way one could not put the right distance between oneself and one's creation. That way one never went beyond the timeliness of a thing.

In the unpublished part of the story "Big Two-Hearted River," a story that was written in 1924, Hemingway enlarged on how true creative writing was quite distinct from what one might have seen or known. Writing about what actually happens, says Hemingway in that piece, was "bad." Invariably such an effort quite killed the experience. The only writing that was any good was what one invented, or "made up," or "imagined." Everything good that he had ever written was what he had made up. Nothing like that had actually happened. He then speaks of the weaknesses of Joyce. Since Dedalus in *Ulysses* was based on Joyce himself, that character was terrible. But Bloom was utter invention, as was Mrs. Bloom. Hence Bloom was "wonderful" and Mrs. Bloom was "the greatest in the world."[6]

Referring to his own work, he asserts that the old man in his story "My Old Man" was totally made up; he had never seen a jockey killed in actual life. He also asserts that Nick Adams in his stories was never based on Hemingway himself. Nick was also made up. But that is how he would like to write; not through tricks, but through talent and imagination. All tricks in course of time turned to clichés; good creative writing never did. Projecting an ideal, Hemingway adds that he would like to write as Cézanne painted.[7]

This section of the story was cut when the story appeared in *In Our Time*, another illustration of aesthetic perception on his part; for though the section is good as far as Hemingway's views on writing go, it blunts the point of the story itself. But these pages clearly show the distinction that Hemingway made between journalism and creative writing, and how journalism was an impediment in the way of true creative writing. A journalist had to unlearn his tricks and learn to invent things, if he wanted to get anywhere as a creative writer.

That is why, whenever he could, Hemingway got away from his official assignments as a journalist and concentrated on his creative work. His personal experiences were of value to him; he did not want to reject them. But he had to add something to them, and perhaps at times to subtract something as well—to take something away to make them readable at the creative level. And it was in those early Paris years that the journalist Hemingway became the artist Hemingway.

Moreover, he was fortunate in the company that he kept there. For every single one of those artists, without exception, was a purist, concerned more with the structure of a work of art, with how a work was put together and how it was made up, than with its contents. Hemingway is not particularly kind to some of them in *A Moveable Feast*, where he says some rather pungent things about them. But the whole of that book is the story of how Hemingway learned to write, and of the likeminded men who helped him along the way.

Hemingway is least gracious about Ford Madox Ford, T. S. Eliot, and Wyndham Lewis. He could not stand Eliot in *The Waste Land* and he thought Wyndham Lewis was a fraud. He is equally unkind about Ford. But the entire work of T. S. Eliot and Wyndham Lewis was a search for perfect structure. As far as Ford Madox Ford was concerned, he was an inspiration to many young writers in the way he spotted their talent and promoted their work. It was he who spotted D. H. Lawrence and published him in the *English Review*. It was he again who spotted the talent of Hemingway (Hemingway's story "Indian Camp" first appeared in Ford's *transatlantic review*). And in the cases of Lawrence and Hemingway, it was the manner of saying the thing that had attracted Ford, not so much the thing itself.[8]

Of the persons that Hemingway liked, there is a long list that includes the names of Gertrude Stein, Harold Loeb, James Joyce, Mike Ward, Scott Fitzgerald, and Ezra Pound. While his affection for others varied, he gives ungrudging praise to Ezra Pound in *A Moveable Feast*. Apparently he liked his personality and his method of work very much. Ronald Duncan in the second volume of his autobiography, *How to Make Enemies*, describes how, when he made a petition to President Eisenhower in the fifties for the release of Ezra Pound, almost every person in the world whom he approached to sign that petition declined. Churchill, Picasso, Bertrand Russell, Smuts, Stravinsky all expressed reservations. T. S. Eliot not only did nothing to help but went to the extent of saying that Ezra should be where he was: "Perhaps in some ways that's the best place for him."[9] Only two artists, says Ronald Duncan, offered to sign without reserve. One of them was Epstein, the other Ernest Hemingway. (Ronald Duncan does not record it, but later, in the Truman period, when Archibald MacLeish organized an appeal for Pound's release, Eliot did help.) Thirty years after he had received benefits at the hands of the master, Hemingway still remembered his debt to him. It was not only a question of the *mot juste*, "the one and only correct word to use"; Ezra Pound was the man who taught him how to stay simple and direct—"the man who had taught me to distrust adjectives."[10]

Hemingway's other artist friends were equally mistrustful of vague themes and flowery adjectives, and were concerned more with the structure and the unity of a work. F. Scott Fitzgerald's objections to the first twenty-eight pages of *The Sun Also Rises* were on the grounds of structure. His unpublished critique of the novel is a remarkable illustration of the aesthetic beliefs and understanding of that period. Fitzgerald speaks of those first pages of *The Sun Also Rises* (later deleted in the published version) as casual and ineffectual. He points out how the worst fault with Hemingway is his trying to entomb in wordiness an anecdote or a joke that might have appealed to him but that has not much meaning in the context of the novel. The first pages of *The Sun Also Rises* contain many such instances and give a feeling of casual showiness to the novel. Then, from the very first page of the novel he picks out at least four phrases of such casualness. He gives a few more illustrations from other pages, and asks, why waste three words saying a thing when one would do? To this, Fitzgerald adds more than twenty instances of what he calls sneers and superiorities and nose-thumbing-at-nothing that disfigure the narrative. It was his duty, he reminds Hemingway, to get rid of these nonessentials. He then gives further illustrations and once again wonders how Hemingway could have written these pages so casually. In the end he talks of clichés that he has found in his prose, and while he admits that the novel is "damn good," he asks him to drastically revise and even cut the first pages.[11]

Edmund Wilson, in the review that he wrote of Hemingway's books for the *Dial* in 1924, noted the influence on Hemingway of Sherwood Anderson and Gertrude Stein. Later in his life Hemingway went on to say tactless things about these two writers. But it is clear from *The Autobiography of Alice B. Toklas* that both of them regarded Hemingway as a product of their influence, and in spite of Hemingway's protests that claim seems to have some basis in reality. Even though Hemingway parodied Anderson in *The Torrents of Spring*, his style and method of story-telling has affinities with Anderson's. As far as Gertrude Stein is concerned, Hemingway was indebted to her in more ways than one.

In another piece, Edmund Wilson remarks that Hemingway was influenced by Gertrude Stein's "conversational as well as her literary style."[12] But more than anything else, he along with the other artists of the twenties owed her the emphasis they all placed on the design of a work, on the method of composition—on the method of the growth of a story.

In the age of New Criticism, Gertrude Stein's essay "Composition as Explanation" deserves a special reconsideration. Along with a few other pieces, this essay was published in her book of the same title by Hogarth Press in 1926. She begins by saying that each age is different from another not in the basic truths of life but in how these truths are viewed and presented. She refers to these components that vary with time as "time sense" (how we look at a thing) and "composition" (how we put together what we look at). That it is mainly a question of technical skill, she leaves one in no doubt: "Each period of living differs from any other period of living not in the way life is but in the way life is conducted and that authentically speaking is composition." She takes time to refer to her book *Three Lives*—the book Edmund Wilson had cited in 1924 as probably having influenced Hemingway. She tells us that in that book she was trying to let her composition form around "a prolonged present." Later she speaks of it as the "continuous present." It was a difficult thing to do, and she records that she began by drastically delimiting her plots, by beginning "again and again with a very small thing." It was out of those small things that she pieced together her bigger works. This was a completely new way of writing, she adds, and war had in a way aided the emergence of the new technique; the war destroyed the old quickly and let the new come in.

Finally in the essay, she speaks of what she terms "equilibration." "That of course means words as well as things and distribution as well as between themselves between the words and themselves and the things and themselves, a distribution as distribution."[13] She also calls it "arrangement." In the closing pages she repeats the statement with which she began her essay: "Nothing changes except composition . . . and the time of and the time in the composition." (Hemingway in his interview with George Plimpton speaks of this as "the abstract relationship of words.")

Close parallels between what Hemingway was trying to do in his work and this essay are quite clear. But the gist of Gertrude Stein's essay is offered here to indicate once again the trend of the age, or at least of the group to which Hemingway belonged. Phrases like "objective correlative," "the *mot juste*," "prolonged present," "equilibration," and "simple declarative sentence" are suggestive of an intense preoccupation with the technique, the method, the craft of composition rather than with its content.

As it happened, Hemingway's editor and lifelong friend Maxwell Perkins turned out to be equally concerned with these very things. He praised Hemingway for the "life" he noticed in his fiction, for its "vitality," and did not ever once suggest a theme to him or applaud him for his themes. When Hemingway in 1928, after he had known Perkins for several years, recommended to him a novel of Morley Callaghan for publication, Perkins turned him down. Perkins wrote to Hemingway on 30 March 1928 to say that they were not accepting Callaghan's novel *Big Boy* as he did not present full-rounded characters. The novel had a sociological rather than fictional interest, concluded Perkins.[14] Once in a while Perkins objected to the use of certain words by Hemingway, but always apologetically, as though he were doing so more to please a few of his anonymous readers. He continued to judge Hemingway on the strength of his artistic skill.

In everything that Hemingway did, he held out the element of luck as a decisive factor in the bargain. The rabbit's foot that he carried in his pocket never served him better than in throwing him into association with such gifted virtuosos.

iii

The closest that Hemingway comes to enunciating his method of composition is in these words: "If it is any use to know it, I always try to write on the principle of the iceberg. There is seven eighths of it under water for every part that shows. Anything you know you can eliminate and it only strengthens your iceberg. It is the part that doesn't show."[15]

Hemingway said this in 1958, three years before his death, in an interview with George Plimpton published in the *Paris Review*. These are exactly the words that Hemingway wrote to Dan Longwell of *Life* magazine in 1952. *Life* was going to publish his *The Old Man and the Sea* in a special issue carrying no advertisements and entirely devoted to the novel. Mr. Longwell had liked the novel and written to Hemingway a highly appreciative letter about what the book did to him and to his wife and to the other people on the *Life* staff who had read the manuscript. In reply Hemingway explained his method of writing, first cautiously, then, when he developed more confidence in the loyalty of Mr. Longwell, more expansively.

Hemingway's first letter, dated 6 July 1952 and thanking Mr. Longwell for his praise of the book, tells him that Hemingway himself has read the novel over two hundred times and each time it had done something to him. He feels that at last he has accomplished what he had been aiming at all his life. He then refers to "The Snows of Kilimanjaro" and says that that is a good story, too, as though in his mind he somehow equated *The Old Man and the Sea* and "The Snows of Kilimanjaro" in terms of intrinsic merit.

Hemingway says nothing more about *The Old Man and the Sea* in that letter, but goes on to add that in order to "win" in "The Snows of Kilimanjaro" he had to throw in the equivalent of "about three divisions." Hemingway here is enunciating one of the two basic attributes of his Iceberg theory—compression (the other one being omission). That is why, he says, the "damned magic" happened in "The Snows." One takes it that that is what he did in *The Old Man and the Sea.* The point seems to be that even though both these tales appeared to be short, Hemingway had compressed things and put more labor into them than works of that length would normally take.[16]

It is in the letter of 27 July 1952 that Hemingway enlarges at length on his technique of composition. The words are identical to those he said to George Plimpton six years later: the principle of the iceberg. He explains, however, that his method is a departure from the method of Naturalism. That is the kind of story in which one includes everything one sees, in order to make it closer to the topographical details in the original. But he says that that method was overworked, and so he wanted to branch out in a newer direction.[17]

Herewith we have Hemingway's complete artistic theory: the iceberg principle projected through (1) compression and (2) controlled omissions. An artist does not have to include in his work everything that he sees. If he knows his material, he can compress details and also safely leave out things he knows too well. His story would acquire strength in proportion to the clever handling of compression and omissions.

Now, this is a very attractive aesthetic theory, but for two snags. First of all, Hemingway was not the originator of the theory; another artist had followed the same method before him. Second, Hemingway by omissions does not quite mean total elimination.

To deal with the other artist first, we see that that was precisely the view held by Rudyard Kipling, and his fiction was constructed on exactly the same aesthetic principle. It is not certain what influence Kipling had on Hemingway, though Hemingway on several occasions praised the older novelist. (We know for certain, however, that Kipling did not care very much for Hemingway's work.[18]) Gertrude Stein once remarked that his poems were "direct and Kiplingesque." But she said nothing about his fiction. No other critic, either, has ever commented on the similarities between them.

But Kipling left a book of memoirs, *Something of Myself,* which was published posthumously in 1937, and the last chapter of that book, entitled "Working-Tools," could as well have been written by Hemingway.

Kipling in that chapter says that since all kinds of postmortems are performed on a writer by critics, once the writer is dead, he is going to reveal his method of composition himself. He takes us into his confidence and tells us that one thing he has really cared for in his life is writing. "The mere act of writing was, and always has been, a physical pleasure to me." It was not easy, however, learning to write. He had to see "that every word should tell, carry, weigh, taste and, if need were, smell." It was all a question of listening to his Daemon, the power within him (Hemingway would have said "Juice"): "Good care I took to walk delicately, lest he should withdraw." Kipling never hurried it, never demanded too much of it, and stopped in time before the power totally ran out. "When your Daemon is in charge, do not try to think consciously. Drift, wait, and obey." Factual details mentioned in a story must of course always be right, and if necessary one must check and verify. As far as was possible he stayed away from "glittering generalities" and would advise other writers to do the same. He gives the example of how once he had foolishly launched such a generality, "East was East and West was West and never the twain should meet," and how for decades he had been misunderstood and misquoted the world around. Then there are references to his personal superstitions regarding the writing material he used and his other working conditions. He always wrote in ink "with a Waverley nib." His pen holder first was "slim, octagonal-sided, agate," and later made of "silver . . . with a quill-like curve." For ink "I demanded the blackest . . . All 'blue-blacks' were an abomination to my Daemon." He speaks of his writing blocks, "large, off-white, blue sheets, of which I was most wasteful." "With a lead pencil I ceased to express— probably because I had to use a pencil in reporting." He never kept diaries or notes of things and people. "If a thing didn't stay in my memory, I argued it was hardly worth writing out." We now have the dimensions of his writing desk: It was "ten feet long from North to South and badly congested." He speaks of certain "gadgets" that he kept handy, on the "work-table." There was a pen tray. A wooden box contained "clips and bands." Another box kept pins. Yet another kept several other small essentials, like screwdrivers. There was also a paper-weight, "said to have been Warren Hastings'." Then there were his other "fetishes"—"a tiny, weighted fur-seal and a leather crocodile."[19]

This chapter of *Something of Myself* makes a fascinating comparative reading alongside Hemingway's interview with George Plimpton, reprinted in *Hemingway and His Critics* edited by Carlos Baker. Both these chapters show how much of writing is the result of hard physical labor, and that the mechanics of what he is writing weighs more heavily with the author than his subject matter. Both Kipling and Hemingway began as journalists and went on to do serious creative work. Both were highly "conscious" artists, aware of the labor of their craft. Both made early successes and names for themselves. Both had their share of fetishes and superstitions.

But the comparison is closest in their method of constructing a tale. We have seen how Hemingway speaks of his "Iceberg" theory—leaving out sections of the story that one knows too well. Kipling too refers to the aesthetic necessity of shortening a tale and leaving out of it things one knows well. The process, he asserts, would increase the force of a story, not lessen it. Kipling thinks that the method partly forced itself on him because of his association with a newspaper office. He began his career on the staff of the *Civil & Military Gazette* of Lahore and later moved on to the *Pioneer* of Allahabad. It was during that period that he started composing fiction, most of which first appeared in these newspapers, particularly the *Pioneer*. Because of the space available, says Kipling, he was obliged to cut his stories. He did that also because he was never through with a tale until he had read it many times, a process which he endearingly calls his "rapturous re-readings."

But he also cut his stories, because he strongly believed that these omissions made the story structurally neater and more powerful. "A tale from which pieces have been raked out is like a fire that has been poked." Like Hemingway, he too declares that these omissions should not be through ignorance. In fact he goes a step further; he asserts that one should first write the whole thing down and then take chunks out of it that one knows too well and that one can otherwise convey. "The excised stuff must have been honestly written for inclusion." Then, when one performs the operation, it will add strength to the story ("like a fire that has been raked"). "One does not know that the operation has been performed, but everyone feels the effect." It is like a magic trick, he adds. "This supports the theory of the chimaera which, having bombinated and been removed, *is* capable of producing secondary causes *in vacuo.*"[20]

So Hemingway was not so original in his structure of the story as we might like to imagine. Evidence of the influence of the one author on the other is not known, nor that of any conscious borrowing. But since Kipling started composing fiction in the 1880s, he must be given the credit of being the first to hit on the form.

iv

Hemingway's originality lies in giving this method a special twist of his own. As has been stated before, he was not a good aesthete in the matter of formulating his creative theories effectively. But what apparently, in contrast to Kipling, he implied by omission was not total deletion but giving certain sections of the narrative a different rhythm.

We know that Hemingway began his career as a creative writer by composing short little vignettes, which were first issued as *in our time,* by the Three Mountains Press in 1923. When the Boni and Liveright edition of *In Our Time* was to be brought out, Hemingway inserted these vignettes alternately in between each separate story. That is how the book of stories, *In Our Time,* stands today. It begins with a vignette, and then there is a short story. Once again there is a vignette and there follows another story. And so it goes.

Now this type of arrangement was not accidental, but by design; it satisfied Hemingway's sense of structure and some need in him for the type of communication he wanted to make to the reader.

Hemingway wrote about it to Edmund Wilson, and

the correspondence is included by the latter in his book *The Shores of Light.* Says Hemingway of this special arrangement of the pieces in *In Our Time,* "That is the way they were meant to go—to give the picture of the whole before examining it in detail."[21] From this description it appears that the vignettes are supposed to give a picture of the "whole," and the stories show the living it out in "detail." Not satisfied, Hemingway elaborates: "like looking with your eyes at something, say a passing coast line, and then looking at it with 15X binoculars." Still not satisfied—"Or rather, maybe, looking at it and then going in and living it—and then coming out and looking at it again."[22]

None of these explanations is satisfactory. The only thing they convey is the apparent concern of the author with two different modes of narration; the satisfactory explanation lies in the two modes that have been shown to develop in the present book. For Hemingway there were always two modes of living: the one the actual happening and the stress and strain of relationships; the other when the individual is by himself. At that moment he is not really living according to a plan. He has surrendered himself to another plan, described incoherently in the letter to Edmund Wilson, but of immense importance to the individual. For it is the second mode that allows him to get the right perspective—a picture of the "whole." The first mode I have called systolic, and the second diastolic. In the first mode the individual is working at a limited level, even though he is working intensely. In the second mode he is exposed to a much larger function of living, a function which includes the individual and yet transcends him and stretches beyond him. It is essentially a mode of passivity. It is also a mode of creativity, for it replenishes the individual, fills him up and gets him ready for further living.

When therefore Hemingway speaks of leaving things out, what he really means by it is rearranging them in a different way and giving them a different rhythm. The very letter of 27 July 1952, in which he expounded his iceberg theory to Mr. Longwell, is helpful in understanding this. Hemingway tells there of how he knew many details of every character in the fishing village to which the old man belonged, but he left that out. He had seen the marlin mate and he left that out. He had also seen a school of more than fifty sperm whales in the same stretch of water and he left that out too.

But he leaves none of these things out, if we look carefully at *The Old Man and the Sea*. He brings them in in a different way.

The details of the village, of the number of men who lived there and the personal life of each one of them, he brings into the story while painting the early morning activity when the fishermen go out to fish. The scene when the old man gets up to go out and there is a muffled sound of feet on the beach, suggesting how men enter their boats and move out to sea, is more effective in giving us the sense of vastness, of the multitude working and suffering, than a pointed and detailed description of these men would have been. The mating of the marlin that Hemingway reports to have seen and then left out is brought into the story of the two marlin that the old man hooked and how the male fish stays with the boat until it has jumped high out of the water and looked at its mate with its own eyes. Regarding the school of fifty sperm whales, the entire sense of numbers, of the organic life in the ocean, that Hemingway conveys—the different species of life that live and die in close proximity to each other—is a transmutation of that early experience.

In all three cases, we observe that nothing has really been left out. When Kipling applied that method, he took whole sections out. But in Hemingway the thing is not deleted; it is included and preserved at a different level or rhythm. Like the vignettes in *In Our Time,* the many men in the fishing village, the mating marlin, and the school of sperm whales, are each transformed in *The Old Man and the Sea* into a diastolic mode to show the old man in passivity, when he is not working, when he is perhaps only looking, or, even better, when he is looking and listening.

It is in this projection of the two-beat method of narration that Hemingway's unique contribution to the structure of fiction lies. By changing the rhythm of the story, he changes the entire meaning of the story. Instead of remaining a tale of action, each of his stories goes on to become a tale of suffering.

Hemingway seemed to have followed the systolic-diastolic pattern in his work habits too. For half of the day he worked, for the other half he lay passive—went out and fished or drank or went on long walks. On surface these activities appear to be "active." But in actuality, Hemingway was waiting for the next burst of creativity, re-creating himself, replenishing the "juice." In the unpublished part of "Big Two-Hearted River," Nick, who is also a writer, speaks of his work habits. He says he would quietly wait for the compulsive moment, when the urge in him would really be great. It was not a matter of "conscience," he tells us. He did not write because he had to, as a chore. It was a question of "peristaltic action."

The phrase peristaltic action again registers the twofold mood. It was a movement which alternated. He had to be passive in order to be active.

Thus, the systolic-diastolic pattern was the aesthetic principle Hemingway had in mind when he spoke of his creative theories. Even though he did not precisely formulate his views, it was a new and a highly effective method of telling a story.

Appendix

Islands in the Stream

(*Note*: The present study was in page proofs when Hemingway's novel *Islands in the Stream* appeared posthumously in the winter of 1970. A few more months elapsed before the novel became available to me in India. In order not to hold up the production of my book any further—it is delayed, as it is—only a brief review of the new novel is given below. For the same reason, most of the quotations from the novel are paraphrased and not given in direct speech—it would have taken too long to secure fresh permission from Hemingway's publishers to quote directly from the novel. Due acknowledgment, however, is made to Charles Scribner's Sons, New York, and Collins, London, for whatever little material is used. This appendix, apart from the main entry, of course, could not be indexed.)

i

When Hemingway died in 1961, there were conflicting reports on the unpublished manuscripts he had left behind. The average reader had no precise idea of these manuscripts until Carlos Baker identified some of them in *Ernest Hemingway, A Life Story*. Later Philip Young and C. W. Mann, with the permission of Mary Hemingway, the novelist's widow, made a formal list of these

211

manuscripts, and the result of their labor, *Hemingway Manuscripts: An Inventory,* threw further light on the material still available in safe deposit vaults.

It seems certain now that Hemingway left two full-length novels, one *The Garden of Eden,* and the other a "Sea" novel, with no precise title for the whole, but with separate titles for the different sections of it: "The Sea When Young," "The Sea When Absent," "The Sea Chase," and "The Sea in Being." "The Sea in Being" was published in Hemingway's lifetime as *The Old Man and the Sea.* The title of the first part was changed by Hemingway to "The Island and the Stream," for Hemingway wrote about it to Charles Scribner in 1951, saying that he was rewriting this section to bring it in line with the quality of the other two parts. It is these three parts of the "Sea" novel that have now been published as *Islands in the Stream.*

The questions that naturally arise in the case of any posthumous publication are: in what shape was the manuscript left by the author, and did he wish to publish the material at all? Till 1951 Hemingway no doubt wanted to bring out the novel, for the letter to Scribner was written in that year. But Hemingway made no reference to the work in the remaining years of his life. What did he do with it in the meantime? Mary Hemingway, in an explanatory note published along with the novel (not included in the British edition), asserts that she and Mr. Charles Scribner, Jr., have worked over the manuscript and have made "some" cuts in the novel. Unfortunately, these emendations and cuts are not indicated in the text itself, something that is usually done when editorial changes are made in the work of a major writer. This gives one an uneasy feeling in passing an opinion on the novel, for one is not sure of the extent of the changes introduced, or of how radically those changes, howsoever small, may have altered the meaning of the author.

But in spite of several reservations about the book, my reading of it indicates that *Islands in the Stream* is an important Hemingway novel. Its worst fault is that its three parts do not "cohere," and apparently Hemingway was never able to perform the revision he had in mind. Yet he must have found much pleasure in writing it, for it effectively projects the symbol that he increasingly adopted in his later writing to indicate his sense of the plurality of life: the symbol of the sea. In his search for an all-embracing sign or emblem that would cover the totality of creation, human and nonhuman life included, whereas he began with the huge, vital symbol of the earth ("One generation passeth away, and another generation cometh; but the earth abideth forever"), he slowly gravitated toward the symbol of the sea, an even more potent figure for the continuous mutation and rhythm of life. Indeed, the two principal symbols that dominate Hemingway's work and overshadow every other are these: *terra firma* and the flowing sea. In *The Sun Also Rises, A Farewell to Arms, For Whom the Bell Tolls,* and in the short stories, the womb of life's pulsation is the solid land; in *To Have and Have Not, Across the River and Into the Trees, The Old Man and the Sea,* and *Islands in the Stream,* it is plainly the moving waters.

As early as 1933, in "Marlin Off the Morro: A Cuban Letter," Hemingway spoke of the sea and the big fish in it in glowing words. Hemingway had known of fish before, but only the river fish, and this was his introduction to the fish of many moods, the hungry fish, the indifferent fish, the playful fish, the angry fish; and this was his introduction to the Gulf Stream. A while later, in 1935, he eulogized the Gulf Stream in a famous passage in *Green Hills of Africa*—"This Gulf Stream you are living with, knowing, learning about, and loving . . ."—a passage I have referred to above in chapter 7. The setting and the action of *Islands in the Stream* are cast in this very Gulf Stream, and, everything apart, the novel shows the attempt Hemingway made to give a fitting aesthetic rendering to the passion of his later life.

ii

The three parts of the novel in its present form are called, respectively, "Bimini," "Cuba," and "At Sea"; they do not have the generic "Sea" titles given by Hemingway. The protagonist is a painter named Thomas Hudson, and he is a characteristic Hemingway hero—extremely sensitive, extremely alive to the life around him, yet extremely lonely and passive, extremely quiescent. In a way this type of hero has been very dear to the American imagination right from the days of James Fenimore Cooper. If Hemingway's novels do not deal with specific American scenes, the short stories do. The characters, particularly the hero, are typically American. But Hemingway places on the solitary hero a new interpretation; instead of seeing him as an instrument of protest and revolt, he sees him as an instrument of meaningful and subtle nonattachment.

When the novel opens, we find Thomas Hudson living a life of solitude on the island of Bimini in the Gulf Stream. Part of his systolic life—his two marriages and divorces—is already behind him, and in fact when we see him first, we see him in a diastolic mood, alone in his luxurious house. (Thomas Hudson is one of Hemingway's few rich heroes.) He is relaxed and unconcerned, for long since he has learned not to worry about things he cannot help. His only preoccupation now is his work as a painter.

The locale for this section is impressive. The house stands on high land, on one side of which is the harbor and on the other the open sea. Soon Thomas Hudson's three sons by his two dissolved marriages, boys called Tom, David, and Andrew, come to visit him during the summer, and the first part describes the life of the father with the children. The boys are well drawn, and are especially appealing since there are very few other accounts of the filial emotion in Hemingway. But on the whole, the first part drags and is slow in gathering momentum; in my opinion it is the weakest section of the three.

To begin with, it suffers from the same defect that marred *Across the River and Into the Trees;* it is too closely autobiographical to allow the novelist room for invention. Thomas Hudson's divorces, number of children, and continued fondness for his first wife run fairly parallel to Hemingway's own life. This in itself is no handicap, if at some stage the fictitious life can separate itself from the actual and function through its independent aesthetic dimensions. That does come to pass, but only at the end of the first part. Till then, the reader is obliged to wade through many pages of tiresome talk neither original nor relevant to the story!

Then again, parts of this first section appear to me to be either derivative from Hemingway's earlier works or to have been used by Hemingway in what he wrote later. His work on this "Sea" novel had started in 1946 and the first draft was completed by 1951, when Hemingway wrote about the book to Charles Scribner. Indications are that Hemingway never returned to the novel for rewriting and alterations. In time, thus, *Islands in the Stream* antedates *The Old Man and the Sea,* which was written following the three parts of the present novel.

An illustration of the material later used by Hemingway is the fishing sequence in the first part, where Thomas Hudson's young son David hooks a big marlin and tries to land it. The action of that sequence in "Bimini" is powerfully told, but Hemingway makes better use of the material, both artistically and speculatively, in *The Old Man and the Sea.* Anyone acquainted with the other novel will readily perceive the similarity in the images and the phrases employed: the fish and the fisher hooked to each other, the fish swimming deep down, the fish pulling the boat out to the sea, the life-and-death struggle of the biological life in the sea, the doubts about who will win, the references to the pain of the fish because the fish "has the hook in his mouth," and the fish finally surfacing, unbelievable as the "length and bulk" are exposed. I would not say that the description in "Bimini" is not different, as well as similar. For example, while the old Santiago fought his battle alone, there are many people to help young David. Also, David's suffering because of the fish is perhaps more touching, since, unlike the old man, he is too young and inexperienced. But then, in the revision, the emphasis should have shifted from the power and glory of the sea and the might of the fish to the suffering of the very, very young. I do not think that that switch is in any way accomplished by the novelist.

As an illustration of the derivative material in this part, the character of Roger Davis seems to me to be based on that of Harry in "The Snows of Kilimanjaro." Roger is a painter-turned-novelist friend of Thomas Hudson and, like his children, is visiting him. He plays absolutely no part in the other two sections of the novel, and is probably used here to bring out the personality of Thomas Hudson, whom he resembles in many ways—a method also employed by Hemingway in *For Whom the Bell Tolls* in creating near twins in Kashkin and Robert Jordan. But Roger's dissatisfaction with his private life, with the mess he has made of his affairs with women, and with his inability to write any more are reminiscent of Harry. (When Roger complains to Thomas Hudson that he can no longer write creatively, Hudson gives him the advice with which the reader of the present book should be familiar: to begin with anything definite and from then on to "make it up," advice that Hemingway himself did not follow in *Across the River and Into the Trees* or in the "Bimini" part of *Islands in the Stream*.)

Then, too, the character of Thomas Hudson, in Part I and the remaining two parts, is to some extent derived from Robert Jordan in *For Whom the Bell Tolls*. Like Robert Jordan, Thomas Hudson plans to live his life by duty—"Get it straight. Your boy you lose. Love you lose. Honor has been gone for a long time. Duty you do." And in both language and thought process he resembles Jordan, particularly in Part I. As Robert Jordan had a few nights with Maria, so Thomas Hudson has five weeks with his children. And in the lisping idiom of Robert Jordan he reflects: "If five weeks is what we get . . . that is what we draw. Five weeks is a good long time to be with people that you love and would wish to be with always."

iii

In addition to the lack of coherence between the three parts of the novel, and to the derivativeness, almost redundancy, of some of its ingredients, there is another disturbing blemish: a measure of sexual inelegance. Perhaps Hemingway had a perverted streak in him all along. I have earlier pointed out how Brett, in chapter 7 of *The Sun Also Rises*, gives Jake Barnes an unnatural sexual satisfaction. In *To Have and Have Not* and *Across the River and Into the Trees*, the human stump is meant to be a phallic symbol. In several of his short stories, lesbian and homosexual relationships are alluded to.

But in all these presentations, Hemingway did not let the unnatural invade the main movement of the story, and none of these descriptions is either explicit or banal. As far as the sexual act is concerned, Hemingway's finesse in dealing with it has already been noted; further, he treated the perversion itself with commendable dignity. In *Islands in the Stream*, however, on three separate occasions—in the Princess episode in Part II, in the account of Thomas Hudson's adventures with the three Chinese girls in Part II, and in Hudson's dream fantasy in Part III, where the .357 Magnum pistol is visualized by him as a phallus—the descriptions are lewd and border on repelling exhibitionism. Aesthetically speaking, this development marks a retrogressive step in Hemingway's total achievement as artist.

iv

The strength of the novel lies in the dignity of the passive hero. There is the life of activity "around" him, but he himself is for the most part inactive. The impetus to the story comes at the end of Part I, when the boys leave their father to return to their respective mothers, and shortly afterwards Hudson receives a telegram saying that the two younger boys, David and Andrew, have been killed in a car accident along with their mother. The blow comes suddenly, and it is from this point that the true Hemingway touch begins. For, as I have stated repeatedly, the art of Hemingway has all along concerned itself not so much with plot as with the *impact* of a certain situation. It may be the flowering of a sudden love, disillusionment in love, or the discovery of a strange secret about someone else (perhaps one's beloved, as in the story "The Sea Change"), or a sudden realization about one's own self. But the event stuns the protagonist into a new type of awareness, and Hemingway's ingenuity lies in making us conscious of the extent of that awareness without verbalizing the new feelings in the form of polemics.

Thomas Hudson had fortified himself in his lonely house and it looked as though nothing could penetrate his defences against hurts of the world. But now comes a new kind of pressure, the loss of his children, and the novel takes shape around the emotion of grief that this gives rise to.

Chapter 15 of Part I is one of enormous diastolic magnitude, in which the fumbling, blinding grief of Hudson is conveyed. We meet him on a ship, six days after the tragedy, making a crossing to Europe, where the boys were killed. He is sitting in his cabin, trying to come to terms with his sorrow but knowing full well that there are no terms one can come to with that emotion. He hopes that time will perhaps cure it. But he also adds that if it is cured by anything less than death, then it is not true sorrow.

Many years pass, and when we next see Hudson in Part II, we are in the Second World War and Hudson is employed to pursue German submarines in the Gulf Stream in his ill-equipped ship. That Hudson has still not recovered from the death of his two youngest boys is shown in a conversation between him and the prostitute,

Honest Lil. Honest Lil is questioning him about the happiest times he has had, and he replies that they were the times when he was either completely alone in the morning as a boy, or when he was with his children—speaking of his children in the plural. But the immediate force for the rest of the story is provided by the death of the third boy, Tom, who, we soon learn, is killed as a pilot over enemy territory. Part II and Part III register for us the vastness of Hudson's grief, where nothing—neither compulsive drinking, nor physical action, nor love-making—will take away the ache of that grief. In the end Hudson himself is mortally wounded and we find him dying on his ship, thus carrying his grief and sorrow to the limits of death.

In my opinion, Part II, entitled "Cuba," is the strongest part of the novel (despite the two scenes of sexual banality already referred to). It has extreme verbal economy, and what more than anything else raises it above the status of the other two parts is that it contains the least amount of derivative stuff; the emotions, as well as the rendering, are altogether fresh and original. The whole section consists of only one long chapter, but it is saturated with details of fine eating and drinking, intelligent repartee, and exquisite miniature portraits of business tycoons, pimps, and faded prostitutes. The description of the prostitute Honest Lil ("Honest" because, though a prostitute, she has a moral code of a kind, by which she lives and which she never trespasses) is the purest and finest of its kind, ranking in artistic perfection with Hemingway's portrayal of Pilar in *For Whom the Bell Tolls*. Then there is a touching encounter of Hudson with Tom's mother in this part, whom it is his unpleasant duty to inform of her boy's death. But above all, the section is infused with the sadness and loneliness of Hudson.

The opening pages, where the cats are described, are superb. The cats serve the same purpose as the big marlin in *The Old Man and the Sea*: they represent for us the larger life of the universe. Like the marlin that Santiago hooks, each of these cats is unique and has a separate personality; Boise, Goats, and Princessa are not so many names; they are so many distinct individualities. Thomas Hudson sleeps with them, shares his meals with them, goes out for walks with them, and so ingenious is the presentation that soon we forget that they are cats and accept them as humans. Even the dead cat, run over by a speeding car on the highway, is made to have a veritable personality through a few carefully chosen sentences. Thomas Hudson tells the cats that there is no answer to the riddle of existence, and in their purring they seem to repeat that back to him.

The scenes and conversations in the bar in Havana, which follow the description of the cats, are equally memorable. It is in a conversation with Honest Lil in that bar that Thomas Hudson gives out what is really eating him. Honest Lil is plying Hudson with drinks and making him talk about his past, in the hope that this will lessen his remorse. But nothing works. Finally Lil asks him cryptically: "Is that it?" and Hudson answers equally cryptically: "That's it." (Honest Lil starts weeping after that.)

In conformity with the practice in Hemingway's other novels, the main emotion of the story is only indirectly stated. But it clearly poses for us the theme of the novel —the sense of grief.

In Part III we see Hudson following the survivors of

a sunken German submarine. This comes immediately after Part II and there is no time lag. But I see both Parts II and III as presentations of the diastolic mood, not of systolic action. The systolic, external action—action for the love of action—takes place only in Part I. The other two sections register the diastolic or the passive action, where what happens—as in the case of Francis Macomber or Manuel Garcia—is a form of reflex to the shock of the boys' death.

Significantly enough, Hemingway details for us Hudson's activities in Part II only after the death of Tom has come to pass. Thus, Hudson's bravado and acts of physical courage, such as once spending nineteen hours on the bridge of his ship without sleep, are indicative only of his reaction to his grief. The same applies to much of his endurance in Part III. For a man of "action" he does rather poorly, for while the rest of his comrades are hunting the enemy, we find Thomas Hudson usually "sleeping." (There are five or six separate sequences when Thomas Hudson is either lying down or is fast asleep, either on the deck of the ship or the beach, right in the midst of danger area.) There are some powerful descriptions of the activity of his men, but he himself is shown generally immobile and passive.

The total effect of Part III is quite strong, but through factors other than Hudson's professed heroism. Its strength comes from the endurance of Thomas Hudson, and from the balancing duality that Hemingway creates between him and his team on the one side and the Germans on the other. The Germans are not treated in the context of the Second World War; reference is hardly made to that war or the conflict that that war might have generated. They are seen by Hemingway as one of the forces in the movement of life. True, Hudson speaks of them as "enemies" and asserts that they cannot escape; but in the same breath he says that neither can "we" escape. There is something larger than both the teams, and that is the endless life-and-death cycle of the total life of the universe, and the mystery of it and the pang of it that Thomas Hudson is unable to fathom. This Part III registers quite effectively.

Summing up, I would rate *Islands in the Stream* as a commendable Hemingway novel. But the pinnacle of his creative glory continues to be *The Old Man and the Sea,* and, to a lesser degree, *The Sun Also Rises* and *A Farewell to Arms.* Indeed, my reading of the new novel further confirms the validity of my stand on Hemingway as formulated in the introductory chapter and the conclusions I arrive at in the rest of the book.

Notes

CHAPTER 1

1. Ernest Hemingway, *Death in the Afternoon* (New York: Charles Scribner's Sons, 1932), p. 2.
2. *Ibid.*
3. Ernest Hemingway, "Monologue to the Maestro: A High Seas Letter," *By-Line: Ernest Hemingway*, ed. William White (New York: Charles Scribner's Sons, 1967), p. 216.
4. Ernest Hemingway, *For Whom the Bell Tolls* (New York, Charles Scribner's Sons, 1940), p. 169.

CHAPTER 2

1. Letter from Ernest Hemingway to Maxwell Perkins, dated 19 November 1926.
2. Ernest Hemingway, *Death in the Afternoon* (New York: Charles Scribner's Sons, 1932), p. 2.
3. Ernest Hemingway, *The Sun Also Rises* (New York: Charles Scribner's Sons, 1926), p. 58.
4. *Ibid.*, p. 207.
5. *Ibid.*, p. 203.
6. *Ibid.*, p. 83.
7. *Ibid.*, p. 247.
8. *Ibid.*, p. 11.
9. Suggested by F. Scott Fitzgerald in his unpublished critique of *The Sun Also Rises*.
10. Malcolm Cowley, "Introduction to *The Sun Also Rises*," *Three Novels of Ernest Hemingway* (New York: Charles Scribner's Sons, 1962), p. xxvii.
11. Ernest Hemingway, *The Sun Also Rises*, p. 20.

12. *Ibid.*, p. 30.
13. *Ibid.*, p. 31.
14. *Ibid.*
15. *Ibid.*, p. 34.
16. T. S. Eliot, *The Complete Poems and Plays* (New York: Harcourt, Brace and Company, 1952), p. 117.
17. Letter from Ernest Hemingway to Bernard Berenson, dated 24 September 1954.
18. Ernest Hemingway, *The Sun Also Rises*, p. 54.
19. *Ibid.*, p. 55.
20. *Ibid.*, p. 247.

CHAPTER 3

1. Leslie A. Fiedler, *Love and Death in the American Novel* (New York: Criterion Books, 1960), pp. 304–5.
2. Ernest Hemingway, *A Farewell to Arms* (New York: Charles Scribner's Sons, 1929), p. 125.
3. Robert Penn Warren, "Introduction to *A Farewell to Arms*," *Three Novels of Ernest Hemingway* (New York: Charles Scribner's Sons, 1962), p. v.
4. Letter from Maxwell Perkins to Ernest Hemingway, dated 24 May 1929.
5. Letter from Ernest Hemingway to Robert Bridges, dated 23 February 1929.
6. Ernest Hemingway, *A Farewell to Arms*, p. 13.
7. *Ibid.*, p. 68.
8. *Ibid.*, p. 199.
9. *Ibid.*, p. 248.
10. Robert Penn Warren, "Introduction to *A Farewell to Arms*," *Three Novels of Ernest Hemingway*, p. ix.
11. Ernest Hemingway, *A Farewell to Arms*, p. 115.
12. *Ibid.*, p. 149.
13. *Ibid.*, p. 293.
14. *Ibid.*, p. 342.
15. Robert W. Lewis, *Hemingway on Love* (Austin and London: University of Texas Press, 1965), pp. 40–54.
16. Ernest Hemingway, *A Farewell to Arms*, p. 31.
17. *Ibid.*
18. *Ibid.*, p. 32.
19. D. H. Lawrence, "Two Ways of Living and Dying," *The Complete*

Poems of D. H. Lawrence, Vol. II, ed. Vivian de Sola Pinto and W. Roberts (London: Heinemann, 1964), p. 675.

20. Ernest Hemingway, *A Farewell to Arms,* p. 39.
21. *Ibid.*
22. *Ibid.,* p. 40.
23. *Ibid.,* p. 44.
24. *Ibid.,* p. 118.
25. *Ibid.,* p. 99.
26. *Ibid.*
27. *Ibid.,* p. 120.
28. *Ibid.,* p. 160.
29. *Ibid.,* p. 111.
30. *Ibid.,* p. 31.
31. *Ibid.,* p. 113.
32. *Ibid.,* p. 122.
33. *Ibid.*
34. *Ibid.,* p. 177.
35. *Ibid.,* p. 266.
36. *Ibid.,* p. 279.
37. *Ibid.,* p. 296.
38. *Ibid.,* p. 320.
39. *Ibid.,* p. 325.
40. *Ibid.,* p. 266.
41. *Ibid.,* p. 267.
42. *Ibid.,* p. 342.
43. *Ibid.,* p. 345.
44. *Ibid.,* p. 350.

CHAPTER 4

1. Leo Gurko, *Ernest Hemingway and the Pursuit of Heroism* (New York: Thomas Y. Crowell, 1968), p. 230.
2. Philip Young, *Ernest Hemingway, A Reconsideration* (University Park and London: Pennsylvania State University Press, 1966), p. 54.
3. *Ibid.,* p. 35.
4. *Ibid.,* p. 63.
5. *Ibid.,* p. 33.
6. *Ibid.* (the last words changed to "face facts" in the present edition. Quoted here as given in the first edition of the book.)
7. Ernest Hemingway, *The Short Stories of Ernest Hemingway* (New York: Charles Scribner's Sons, 1938), p. 227.

8. *Ibid.*, p. 94.
9. *Ibid.*, p. 95.
10. *Ibid.*, p. 102.
11. *Ibid.*, p. 287.
12. *Ibid.*, p. 288.
13. *Ibid.*, p. 8.
14. *Ibid.*, p. 12.
15. *Ibid.*, p. 23.
16. *Ibid.*, p. 36.
17. Philip Young, *Ernest Hemingway, A Reconsideration*, p. 47.
18. Malcolm Cowley, "Hemingway at Midnight," *New Republic* 3, No. 7 (14 August 1944): 192.
19. Philip Young, *Ernest Hemingway, A Reconsideration*, p. 45.
20. Ernest Hemingway, *Green Hills of Africa* (New York: Charles Scribner's Sons, 1935), p. 26.
21. Malcolm Cowley, "Hemingway at Midnight," *New Republic*, p. 192.
22. Ernest Hemingway, *The Short Stories of Ernest Hemingway*, p. 210.
23. *Ibid.*
24. *Ibid.*, p. 212.
25. *Ibid.*, p. 213.
26. *Ibid.*, p. 214.
27. *Ibid.*, p. 215.
28. *Ibid.*
29. *Ibid.*
30. *Ibid.*, p. 227.
31. *Ibid.*, p. 147.
32. *Ibid.*, p. 54.
33. *Ibid.*
34. *Ibid.*, p. 60.
35. *Ibid.*, p. 66.
36. *Ibid.*, p. 64.
37. *Ibid.*
38. *Ibid.*, p. 67.
39. *Ibid.*
40. *Ibid.*
41. *Ibid.*, p. 71.
42. *Ibid.*, p. 73.
43. *Ibid.*, p. 74.
44. *Ibid.*
45. *Ibid.*
46. *Ibid.*
47. *Ibid.*, p. 76.

CHAPTER 5

1. Carlos Baker, *Ernest Hemingway, A Life Story* (New York: Charles Scribner's Sons, 1969), pp. 276–82.
2. *Ibid.*, p. 316.
3. *Ibid.*, p. 338.
4. *Ibid.*, p. 371.
5. Ernest Hemingway, *For Whom the Bell Tolls* (New York: Charles Scribner's Sons, 1940), p. 8.
6. *Ibid.*, p. 45.
7. *Ibid.*, p. 2.
8. *Ibid.*, p. 4.
9. *Ibid.*, p. 17.
10. *Ibid.*, p. 39.
11. *Ibid.*, p. 43.
12. *Ibid.*
13. *Ibid.*, p. 196.
14. *Ibid.*, p. 303.
15. *Ibid.*, p. 304.
16. *Ibid.*
17. *Ibid.*, p. 196.
18. *Ibid.*, p. 339.
19. *Ibid.*, p. 43.
20. *Ibid.*, p. 66.
21. *Ibid.*, p. 91.
22. *Ibid.*, p. 164.
23. *Ibid.*
24. Carlos Baker, *Hemingway, The Writer as Artist* (Princeton: Princeton University Press, 1952), pp. 246–50.
25. Arturo Barea, "Not Spain but Hemingway," *Hemingway and His Critics*, ed. Carlos Baker (New York: Hill and Wang, 1961), pp. 202–12.
26. Ernest Hemingway, *For Whom the Bell Tolls*, p. 390.
27. *Ibid.*
28. *Ibid.*, p. 391.
29. *Ibid.*, p. 89.
30. *Ibid.*
31. *Ibid.*, p. 56.
32. *Ibid.*, p. 88.
33. *Ibid.*, p. 92.
34. *Ibid.*, p. 90.

35. *Ibid.,* p. 97.
36. *Ibid.,* p. 153.
37. *Ibid.*
38. *Ibid.,* p. 154.
39. *Ibid.*
40. *Ibid.,* p. 155.
41. *Ibid.,* p. 156.
42. *Ibid.,* p. 172.
43. *Ibid.,* p. 166.
44. *Ibid.,* p. 169.
45. *Ibid.*
46. *Ibid.,* p. 73.
47. *Ibid.,* p. 167.
48. *Ibid.,* p. 73.
49. *Ibid.*
50. *Ibid.,* p. 393.
51. *Ibid.,* p. 463.
52. *Ibid.,* p. 466.
53. *Ibid.,* p. 467.
54. *Ibid.*

CHAPTER 6

1. Letter from Ernest Hemingway to Major General Charles T. Lanham, dated 14 April 1945.
2. Letter from Ernest Hemingway to Major General Charles T. Lanham, dated 18 January 1950.
3. Ernest Hemingway, *Across the River and Into the Trees* (New York: Charles Scribner's Sons, 1950), p. 13.
4. *Ibid.,* p. 241.
5. *Ibid.,* p. 10.
6. *Ibid.,* p. 27.
7. *Ibid.,* p. 33.
8. Ernest Hemingway, *The Sun Also Rises* (New York: Charles Scribner's Sons, 1926), p. 31.
9. Ernest Hemingway, *A Farewell to Arms* (New York: Charles Scribner's Sons, 1929), p. 58.
10. Ernest Hemingway, *Across the River and Into the Trees*, p. 64.
11. *Ibid.,* p. 84.
12. *Ibid.,* p. 85.
13. *Ibid.,* p. 112.
14. *Ibid.,* p. 111.

15. *Ibid.*, p. 135.
16. *Ibid.*, p. 151.
17. *Ibid.*, p. 158.
18. *Ibid.*, p. 7.
19. *Ibid.*, p. 9.
20. *Ibid.*, p. 24.
21. *Ibid.*, p. 31.
22. *Ibid.*, p. 65.
23. *Ibid.*, p. 68.
24. *Ibid.*, p. 149.
25. *Ibid.*, p. 151.
26. *Ibid.*, p. 228.
27. *Ibid.*, p. 245.
28. *Ibid.*, p. 252.
29. *Ibid.*, p. 217.
30. *Ibid.*, p. 251.
31. *Ibid.*, p. 63.
32. *Ibid.*, p. 123.
33. *Ibid.*, p. 165.
34. *Ibid.*, p. 230.

CHAPTER 7

1. Letter from Ernest Hemingway to Wallace Meyer, dated 4 March 1952.
2. Robert P. Weeks, "Fakery in *The Old Man and the Sea*," *Twentieth Century Interpretations of* The Old Man and the Sea, ed. Katharine T. Jobes (Englewood Cliffs: Prentice-Hall, 1968), pp. 34–40.
3. Dwight Macdonald, "Ernest Hemingway," *Encounter* 18, no. 1 (January 1962): 117.
4. Katharine T. Jobes, "Introduction," *Twentieth Century Interpretations of* The Old Man and the Sea, p. 2.
5. Ernest Hemingway, *The Old Man and the Sea* (New York: Charles Scribner's Sons, 1952), p. 137.
6. *Ibid.*, p. 127.
7. *Ibid.*, p. 33.
8. *Ibid.*, p. 67.
9. *Ibid.*, p. 99.
10. *Ibid.*, p. 25.
11. *Ibid.*, p. 138.
12. *Ibid.*, p. 29.
13. A. R. Wells, "A Ritual of Transfiguration: *The Old Man and the*

Sea," *Twentieth Century Interpretations of* The Old Man and the Sea, p. 62.

14. *Ibid.,* p. 63.
15. Ernest Hemingway, *The Old Man and the Sea,* p. 75.
16. *Ibid.,* p. 110.
17. *Ibid.,* p. 114.
18. *Ibid.,* p. 36.
19. *Ibid.,* p. 15.
20. *Ibid.,* p. 25.
21. *Ibid.,* p. 9.
22. *Ibid.,* p. 136.
23. *Ibid.,* p. 10.
24. *Ibid.,* p. 14.
25. *Ibid.,* p. 32.
26. *Ibid.*
27. *Ibid.,* p. 33.
28. *Ibid.,* p. 32.
29. *Ibid.,* p. 34.
30. *Ibid.,* p. 41.
31. *Ibid.,* p. 55.
32. *Ibid.,* p. 114.
33. *Ibid.,* p. 61.
34. *Ibid.,* p. 43.
35. *Ibid.,* p. 45.
36. *Ibid.,* p. 62.
37. *Ibid.,* p. 105.
38. *Ibid.,* p. 112.
39. *Ibid.,* p. 73.
40. *Ibid.,* p. 27.
41. Ernest Hemingway, *Green Hills of Africa* (New York: Charles Scribner's Sons, 1935), p. 148.
42. *Ibid.*
43. *Ibid.,* p. 149.
44. *Ibid.,* p. 150.
45. *Ibid.,* p. 149.

CHAPTER 8

1. Letter from Ernest Hemingway to Wallace Meyer, dated 28 November 1952.
2. Edmund Wilson, *The Shores of Light* (New York: Farrar, Straus and Young, 1952), p. 121.

3. Letter from Ernest Hemingway to Miss Janet Flanner, dated 18 April 1933.

4. Ernest Hemingway, *Death in the Afternoon* (New York: Charles Scribner's Sons, 1932), p. 2.

5. Ernest Hemingway, "Monologue to the Maestro: A High Seas Letter," *By-Line: Ernest Hemingway*, ed. William White (New York: Charles Scribner's Sons, 1967), p. 216.

6. Ernest Hemingway, "Deleted Portion of 'Big, Two-Hearted River.'" Unpublished manuscript.

7. *Ibid.*

8. Ford Madox Ford, *Portraits from Life* (Boston: Houghton Mifflin, 1937), pp. 70–89 and *It was the Nightingale* (Philadelphia: Lippincott, 1933), p. 323, respectively.

9. Ronald Duncan, *How to Make Enemies* (London: Rupert Hart-Davis, 1968), p. 327.

10. Ernest Hemingway, *A Moveable Feast* (New York: Charles Scribner's Sons, 1964), p. 134.

11. F. Scott Fitzgerald, "Critique of *The Sun Also Rises*." Unpublished manuscript.

12. Edmund Wilson, *The Shores of Light*, p. 577.

13. Gertrude Stein, *Composition as Explanation* (London: Hogarth Press, 1926), pp. 5–30.

14. Letter from Maxwell Perkins to Ernest Hemingway, dated 30 March 1928.

15. George Plimpton, "An Interview with Ernest Hemingway," *Hemingway and His Critics*, ed. Carlos Baker (New York: Hill and Wang, 1961), p. 34.

16. Letter from Ernest Hemingway to Dan Longwell, dated 6 July 1952.

17. Letter from Ernest Hemingway to Dan Longwell, dated 27 July 1952.

18. Letter from Owen Wister to Maxwell Perkins, dated 18 February 1929.

19. Rudyard Kipling, *Something of Myself* (New York: Doubleday, Doran & Co., 1937), pp. 221–48.

20. *Ibid.*, p. 224.

21. Edmund Wilson, *The Shores of Light*, p. 122.

22. *Ibid.*, p. 123.

Select Bibliography

BIBLIOGRAPHIES OF ERNEST HEMINGWAY

Cohn, Louis Henry. *A Bibliography of the Works of Ernest Hemingway*. New York: Random House, 1931.

Hanneman, Audre. *Ernest Hemingway; a Comprehensive Bibliography*. Princeton: Princeton University Press, 1967.

Samuels, Lee. *A Hemingway Check List*. With a preface by Ernest Hemingway. New York: Charles Scribner's Sons, 1951.

STUDIES OF ERNEST HEMINGWAY

Aldridge, John W. *After the Lost Generation: A Critical Study of the Writers of Two Wars*. New York: McGraw-Hill, 1951, pp. 23–43, 107–16.

Algren, Nelson. *Notes from a Sea Diary: Hemingway All the Way*. New York: Putnam, 1965.

Arnold, Lloyd R. *High on the Wild with Hemingway*. Caldwell, Idaho: Caxton Printers, 1968.

Aronowitz, Alfred G. and Peter Hamill. *Ernest Hemingway: The Life and Death of a Man*. New York: Lancer Books, 1961.

Asselineau, Roger, ed. *The Literary Reputation of Ernest Hemingway in Europe*. Paris: Minard, Lettres Modernes, 1965.

Atkins, John Alfred. *The Art of Ernest Hemingway; His Work and Personality*. London: Peter Nevill, 1952.

Baker, Carlos. *Hemingway: The Writer as Artist*. Princeton: Princeton University Press, 1952.

———. *Hemingway and His Critics: An International Anthology*. New York: Hill & Wang, 1961.

————, ed. *Ernest Hemingway: Critiques of Four Major Novels.* New York: Charles Scribner's Sons, 1962.

————. *Ernest Hemingway, A Life Story.* New York: Charles Scribner's Sons, 1969.

Baker, Sheridan Warner. *Ernest Hemingway: An Introduction and Interpretation.* New York: Holt, Rinehart & Winston, 1967.

Bates, H. E. *The Modern Short Story: A Critical Survey.* London: Thomas Nelson, 1941, pp. 96–97, 167–78.

Beach, Joseph Warren. *The Outlook for American Prose.* Chicago: University of Chicago Press, 1926, pp. 277–78.

————. *The Twentieth Century Novel: Studies in Technique.* New York: Appleton-Century-Crofts, 1932, pp. 532–37.

————. *American Fiction: 1920–1940.* New York: Macmillan, 1941, pp. 69–93, 97–119.

Beach, Sylvia. *Shakespeare and Company.* New York: Harcourt, Brace, 1959, pp. 77–83.

Benson, Jackson J. *Hemingway; The Writer's Art of Self-defence.* Minneapolis: University of Minnesota Press, 1969.

Biles, J. I. *The Aristotelian Structure of* A Farewell to Arms. Atlanta: Georgia State College, 1965.

Booth, Wayne C. *The Rhetoric of Fiction.* Chicago: University of Chicago Press, 1961, pp. 151–52, 199–300.

Brinnin, John Malcolm. *The Third Rose: Gertrude Stein and Her World.* Boston: Atlantic-Little, Brown, 1959, pp. 249–263.

Brooks, Cleanth and Robert Penn Warren. *Understanding Fiction.* New York: Appleton-Century-Crofts, 1943, pp. 316–25.

Brooks, Cleanth. *The Hidden God: Studies in Hemingway, Faulkner, Yeats, Eliot and Warren.* New Haven: Yale University Press, 1963, pp. 6–21.

Brooks, Van Wyck. *The Confident Years: 1885–1915.* New York: E. P. Dutton Co., 1952, pp. 570–76.

Burgum, Edwin Berry. *The Novel and the World's Dilemma.*

New York: Oxford University Press, 1947, pp. 184–204.

Burnett, Whit. *The Literary Life and the Hell with It.* New York: Harper, 1939, pp. 173–78, 198–99.

Callaghan, Morley. *That Summer in Paris: Memories of Tangled Friendships with Hemingway, Fitzgerald, and some others.* New York: Coward-McCann, 1963.

Connolly, Cyril. *Enemies of Promise.* London: Routledge, 1938; this edition Boston: Little, Brown and Co., Inc., 1939, pp. 80–85.

———. *Previous Convictions.* London: Hamish Hamilton, 1963, pp. 290–98.

———. *The Modern Movement: One Hundred Key Books from England, France and America, 1880–1950.* London: Hamish Hamilton, 1966.

DeFalco, Joseph. *The Hero in Hemingway's Short Stories.* Pittsburgh: University of Pittsburgh Press, 1963.

Eastman, Max. *Great Companions: Critical Memoirs of Some Famous Friends.* New York: Farrar, Straus & Cudahy, 1959, pp. 41–76.

Edgar, Pelham. *The Art of the Novel: From 1700 to the Present Time.* New York: Macmillan, 1933, pp. 338–51.

Fenton, Charles A. *The Apprenticeship of Ernest Hemingway: The Early Years.* New York: Farrar, Straus & Young, 1954.

Fiedler, Leslie A. *Love and Death in the American Novel.* New York: Criterion Books, 1960, pp. 304–9, 350–52.

———. *Waiting for the End.* New York: Stein & Day, 1964, pp. 9–19.

Fitzgerald, F. Scott. *The Letters of F. Scott Fitzgerald.* Ed. Andrew Turnbull. New York: Charles Scribner's Sons, 1963, pp. 295–313.

Geismar, Maxwell. *Writers in Crisis: The American Novel Between Two Wars.* Boston: Houghton Mifflin Co., 1942, pp. 39–85.

———. *American Moderns: From Rebellion to Conformity.* New York: Hill & Wang, 1958, pp. 54–64.

Gibbs, Wolcott. *Bed of Neuroses*. New York: Dodd, Mead, 1937, pp. 261–65.

Goldhurst, William. *F. Scott Fitzgerald and His Contemporaries*. Cleveland: World Publishing Co., 1963, pp. 155–216.

Gordon, Caroline. *How to Read a Novel*. New York: Viking Press, 1957, pp. 99–102, 146–47.

Grant, Douglas. *Purpose and Place: Essays on American Writers*. London: Macmillan, 1965, pp. 169–82.

Graves, Robert and Alan Hodge. *The Reader Over Your Shoulder: A Handbook for Writers of Prose*. New York: Macmillan Company, 1944, pp. 304–6.

Gurko, Leo. *Heroes, Highbrows and the Popular Mind*. Indianapolis: Bobbs-Merrill, 1953. pp. 186–87, 270–72.

———. *Ernest Hemingway and the Pursuit of Heroism*. New York: Crowell, 1968.

Hale, Nancy. *The Realities of Fiction: A Book About Writing*. Boston: Little, Brown, 1962, pp. 85–112.

Hanemann, H. W. *The Facts of Life: A Book of Brighter Biography Executed in the Manner of Some of Our Best or Best-Known Writers*. New York: Farrar & Rinehart, 1930, pp. 131–59.

Hartwick, Harry. *The Foreground of American Fiction*. New York: American Book, 1934, pp. 151–59.

Hemingway, Leicester. *My Brother, Ernest Hemingway*. Cleveland: World, 1962.

Herrmann, Lazar. *Hemingway; A Pictorial Biography*. New York: Viking Press, 1961.

Hoffman, Frederick J. *The Twenties: American Writing in the Postwar Decade*. New York: Viking Press, 1955, pp. 66–76, 80–85.

Hotchner, A. E. *Papa Hemingway: A Personal Memoir*. New York: Random House, 1966.

Hovey, Richard Bennett. *Hemingway: The Inward Terrain*. Seattle: University of Washington Press, 1968.

Howe, Irving. *A World More Attractive: A View of Modern*

Literature and Politics. New York: Horizon Press, 1963, pp. 59–76.

Isabelle, Julanne. *Hemingway's Religious Experience.* New York: Vantage Press, 1964.

Jobes, Katharine T., ed. *Twentieth Century Interpretations of The Old Man and the Sea.* Englewood Cliffs, N.J.: Prentice-Hall, 1968.

Joost, Nicholas. *Ernest Hemingway and the Little Magazines: The Paris Years.* Barre, Mass.: Barre Pub., 1968.

Kiley, John Gerald. *Hemingway: A Title Fight in Ten Rounds.* London: Methuen, 1965.

Killinger, John. *Hemingway and the Dead Gods: A Study in Existentialism.* Lexington: University of Kentucky Press, 1960.

Land, Myrick. *The Fine Art of Literary Mayhem: A Lively Account of Famous Writers and Their Feuds.* New York: Holt, Rinehart & Winston, 1962, pp. 180–204.

Lawrence, D. H. *Phoenix: The Posthumous Papers of D. H. Lawrence.* Ed. Edward D. McDonald. London: Heinemann, 1936, p. 365.

Legman, Gershon. *Love and Death: A Study in Censorship.* New York: Breaking Point, 1949, pp. 86–90.

Lewis, Robert William. *Hemingway on Love.* Austin and London: University of Texas Press, 1965.

Lewis, Wyndham. *Men Without Art.* London: Cassell, 1934, pp. 17–40.

Linn, James Weber and H. W. Taylor. *A Foreword to Fiction.* New York: D. Appleton-Century, 1935, pp. 112–13.

Loeb, Harold. *The Way It Was.* New York: Criterion, 1959, pp. 190–94, 285–98.

McCaffery, John K.M., ed. *Ernest Hemingway: The Man and His Work.* Cleveland and New York: World, 1950.

McCole, C. John. *Lucifer at Large.* London and New York: Longmans, Green, 1937, pp. 153–72.

Macdonald, Dwight. *Against the American Grain: Essays on the Effects of Mass Culture.* New York: Random House, 1962, pp. 167–184.

Machlin, Milt. *The Private Hell of Hemingway.* New York: Paperback Library, 1962.

Mallett, Richard. *Literary Upshots or Split Reading.* London: Jonathan Cape, 1951, pp. 44–47.

Meaker, M. J. *Sudden Endings.* New York: Doubleday, 1964, pp. 1–25.

Mizener, Arthur. *The Sense of Life in the Modern Novel.* Boston: Houghton Mifflin, 1964, pp. 205–226.

Montgomery, Constance Cappel. *Hemingway in Michigan.* New York: Fleet, 1966.

Morris, Wright. *The Territory Ahead.* New York: Harcourt, Brace, 1958, pp. 133–46.

Moseley, E. M. *Pseudonyms of Christ in the Modern Novel: Motifs and Methods.* Pittsburgh: University of Pittsburgh Press, 1962, pp. 205–13.

Muller, Herbert J. *Modern Fiction: A Study of Values.* New York: Funk & Wagnalls, 1937, pp. 383–403.

Noble, David W. *The Eternal Adam and the New World Garden; The Central Myth in the American Novel Since 1830.* New York: George Braziller, 1968, pp. 133–60.

O'Connor, Frank. *The Lonely Voice: A Study of the Short Story.* Cleveland: World, 1963, pp. 156–69.

O'Connor, William Van. *The Grotesque: An American Genre and Other Essays.* Carbondale: Southern Illinois University Press, 1962, pp. 119–24.

O'Faolain, Sean. *The Vanishing Hero: Studies in Novelists of the Twenties.* London: Eyre & Spottiswoode, 1956, pp. 137–65.

O'Hara, John. *Sweet and Sour: Comments on Books and People.* New York: Random House, 1954, pp. 39–44.

Rahv, Philip. *Image and Idea: Twenty Essays on Literary Themes.* New York: New Directions, 1957, pp. 188–95.

Rosenfeld, Isaac. *An Age of Enormity: Life and Writing in the Forties and Fifties.* Ed. Theodore Solotaroff. Cleveland: World, 1962, pp. 258–67.

Rosenfeld, Paul. *By Way of Art: Criticism of Music, Literature,*

Painting, Sculpture and the Dance. New York: Coward-McCann, 1928, pp. 151–63.

Ross, Lillian. *Portrait of Hemingway.* New York: Simon & Schuster, 1961.

Rovit, Earl H. *Ernest Hemingway.* New York: Twayne, 1963.

Rubin, Louis D., Jr. *The Teller in the Tale.* Seattle & London: University of Washington Press, 1967, pp. 129–32.

Sanderson, Stewart. *Ernest Hemingway.* Edinburgh: Oliver & Boyd, 1961.

Sanford, Marcelline Hemingway. *At the Hemingways: A Family Portrait.* Boston: Atlantic-Little, Brown, 1962.

Savage, Derek S. *The Withered Branch: Six Studies in the Modern Novel.* London: Eyre & Spottiswoode, 1950, pp. 23–43.

Schorer, Mark. *The World We Imagine, Selected Essays.* New York: Farrar, Straus & Giroux, 1968, pp. 299–382.

Scott, Nathan A. *Ernest Hemingway, A Critical Essay.* Grand Rapids: Eerdmans, 1966.

Seward, William Ward. *My Friend Ernest Hemingway; An Affectionate Reminiscence.* South Brunswick: A. S. Barnes and Company, 1969.

Singer, Kurt Deutsch. *Ernest Hemingway: Life and Death of a Giant.* Los Angeles: Holloway House, 1961.

―――― and Jane Sherrod. *Ernest Hemingway, Man of Courage: A Biographical Sketch of a Nobel Prize Winner in Literature.* Minneapolis: Denison, 1963.

Snell, George. *The Shapers of American Fiction: 1798–1947.* New York: Dutton, 1947, pp. 156–72.

Spivey, Ted R. *Religious Themes in Two Modern Novelists.* Atlanta: Georgia State College, 1965.

Stein, Gertrude. *The Autobiography of Alice B. Toklas.* New York: Harcourt, Brace, 1933, pp. 261–71.

Stephens, Robert O. *Hemingway's Nonfiction; The Public Voice.* Chapel Hill: University of North Carolina Press, 1968.

Stone, Edward. *A Certain Morbidness, A View of American*

Literature. Carbondale: Southern Illinois University Press, 1969, pp. 161–63.

Tanner, Tony. *The Reign of Wonder: Naivety and Reality in American Literature.* Cambridge: Cambridge University Press, 1965, pp. 228–57.

Wagenknecht, Edward C. *Cavalcade of the American Novel.* New York: Holt, 1952, pp. 368–81.

Walcutt, Charles. *American Literary Naturalism, A Divided Stream.* Minneapolis: University of Minnesota Press, 1956, pp. 270–80.

Warren, Robert Penn. *Selected Essays.* New York, Random House, 1958, pp. 80–118.

Weeks, Robert Percy, ed. *Hemingway: A Collection of Critical Essays.* Englewood Cliffs, N.J.: Prentice-Hall, 1962.

White, E. B. *The Second Tree from the Corner.* New York: Harper, 1954, pp. 140–143.

Wilson, Colin. *The Outsider.* London: Gollancz, 1956, pp. 31–39.

Wilson, Edmund. *The Shores of Light: A Literary Chronicle of the Twenties and Thirties.* New York: Farrar, Straus & Young, 1952, pp. 115–24, 339–44, 616–29.

Woolf, Virginia. *Granite and Rainbow: Essays.* New York: Harcourt, Brace, 1958, pp. 85–92.

Young, Philip. *Ernest Hemingway.* New York and Toronto: Rinehart, 1952.

————. *Ernest Hemingway.* Minneapolis: University of Minnesota Press, 1959.

————. *Ernest Hemingway, A Reconsideration.* University Park and London, Pennsylvania State University Press, 1966. (A reissue of Philip Young's *Ernest Hemingway,* 1952, with additional material.)

Index

Action, cycles of systolic-diastolic, 19, 23–26, 30, 32, 34–36, 37–40, 46–48, 51, 88, 94, 97–101, 105–8, 110–18, 132–33, 137, 143–44, 162, 183–86, 206–7, 209
Action, Hemingway's meaning, 18–19
Anderson, Sherwood, 197
Anti-heroes, 19

Baker, Carlos, 18, 32, 80, 86, 121, 131, 203
Beauty, 66–67
Bennett, Arnold, 19
Berenson, Bernard, 42
Bergson, Henri, 41–42
"Big wound," 154–60
Blake, William, 164, 172–73
Bridges, Robert, 52

Caesuras, 23–25, 59, 63, 74, 86, 101ff, 137–38, 149, 160, 168
Callaghan, Morley, 199
Camus, Albert, 19–21
Cézanne, Paul, 194
Churchill, Winston, 195
Coleridge, Samuel T., 178–79
Communism, 121
Connolly, Cyril, 171
Correspondence, Hemingway's, 191
Cowley, Malcolm, 34, 102, 104, 151

Diastolic action. *See* action, cycles of
Dickens, Charles, 31
Donne, John, 123, 130, 148
Duncan, Ronald, 195–96
Dunne, J. W., 38

Eastern art, 60
Eliot, T. S., 28–29, 41, 71, 195–96
Emerson, Ralph W., 45
Empson, William, 28
Epic, 31

Faulkner, William, 28–29
Fenton, Charles A., 192
Fiedler, Leslie, 49, 60–61, 68
Fielding, Henry, 103
Fitzgerald, F. Scott, 191, 195–96
Flanner, Janet, 191
Ford, Ford Madox, 195
Forster, E. M., 158
Fusion, 181–82, 187–88

Galsworthy, John, 19
Gurko, Leo, 80

Hardy, Thomas, 173
Hawthorne, Nathaniel, 26, 77
Hemingway, Ernest
    WORKS
    Across the River and Into the Trees, 110, 150–69, 175
    Death in the Afternoon, 18, 109, 151

Farewell to Arms, A, 49–79, 124–25, 130, 148, 154, 158

Fifth Column, The, 122–23

For Whom the Bell Tolls, 26, 72, 120–49, 152, 156, 158, 160, 167

Green Hills of Africa, 18, 103, 151, 188

In Our Time, 81–82, 194, 205

Islands in the Stream, 211–23

Men Without Women, 81

Moveable Feast, A, 151, 162, 195

Old Man and the Sea, The, 78, 110, 121, 150, 163, 170–89, 200, 207

Sun Also Rises, The, 28–48, 49–50, 61, 69, 72, 121, 125, 130, 155–56, 158, 196

To Have and Have Not, 122, 132–33, 157, 159

Torrents of Spring, The, 197

Winner Take Nothing, 81

SHORT STORIES

"Battler, The," 87

"Big Two-Hearted River," 101–8, 193, 208

"Cat in the Rain," 87, 109

"Clean, Well-Lighted Place, A," 83, 87

"Day's Wait, A," 84

"Doctor and the Doctor's Wife, The," 82, 84–85, 87, 90–93

"End of Something, The," 83, 87, 108

"Fathers and Sons," 87

"Fifty Grand," 87, 109

"Gambler, the Nun, and the Radio, The," 84

"Homage to Switzerland," 83–84

"Hills Like White Elephants," 87, 109

"Indian Camp," 72, 82, 87–91, 93, 105

"Killers, The," 72, 87, 93–94

"Light of the World, The," 83

"Mr. and Mrs. Elliot," 87

"Mother of a Queen, The," 84

"My Old Man," 87, 109, 194

"Natural History of the Dead, A," 84

"Now I Lay Me," 83, 109

"One Reader Writes," 87

"Sea Change, The," 84, 87, 109

"Short Happy Life of Francis Macomber, The," 84, 87, 95–101

"Snows of Kilimanjaro, The," 84, 87, 94, 109–18, 128, 160, 188, 200

"Soldier's Home," 83, 87, 108

"Ten Indians," 87

"Undefeated, The," 87, 95, 100, 172

"Very Short Story, A," 83

"Wine of Wyoming," 84

Heroes, 23, 29, 50, 54, 80–81, 83, 85, 96, 102–3, 118, 144, 165, 183; passivity of, 23, 50, 118, 165, 183. *See also* passivity, creative

Homer, 103–4

Huxley, Aldous, 45

Iceberg theory, 200–205, 208

India, 71

Inventiveness, 150–51

Italicized passages, 110, 113

Jacobs, Katherine T., 171

James, Henry, 17, 19–20

Journalism, 121, 192–94, 203

Joyce, James, 20, 28, 41, 193, 195

Kalidasa, 60
Keats, John, 191
Kipling, Rudyard, 201–5, 208

Lanham, Charles T., 152, 191
Lawrence, D. H., 17, 31, 41–42, 144–45, 191, 195
Leavis, F. R., 77
Lewis, Wyndham, 195
Loeb, Harold, 195
Longwell, Dan, 200, 207
Lost-generation theory rejected, 29

Macdonald, Dwight, 171
MacLeish, Archibald, 196
Melville, Herman, 26–27, 77
Meyer, Wallace, 190
Mysticism, 109, 119, 144, 147

Narrative method, Hemingway's description, 199–200. See also iceberg theory
Nick Adams, general explanation, 81
Nihilism, 150

Passivity, creative, 19, 21, 39, 43, 58, 94, 107
Pauses. See caesuras
Perkins, Maxwell, 29, 51–52, 191, 199
Pessimism theory rejected, 93
Picasso, Pablo, 195
Plato, 66
Plimpton, George, 198, 200–201, 203
Plurality of life, 172
Poe, Edgar Allan, 26–27, 177
Pound, Ezra, 195–96
Princeton University, 152
Prose, the "fifth dimension," 103–4

Psychological novelists, 19
Public image, Hemingway's, 152–53

Religiosity, 45, 146–47, 149
Remarque, Erich Maria, 56
Resignation theme, 173, 186
Ross, Lilian, 151
Russell, Bertrand, 195

Sartre, Jean-Paul, 19
Shakespeare, William, 81
Smart, David, 123
Smuts, Jan Christiaan, 195
Stein, Gertrude, 29, 195, 197–99, 202
Stevens, Wallace, 116–17
Stravinsky, Igor, 195
Systolic action. See action, cycles of

Tolstoy, Leo, 56, 72
Toynbee, Philip, 171
Trauma theory rejected, 54–55, 62
Twain, Mark, 26

Ward, T. H. (Mike), 195
Warren, Robert Penn, 17, 51, 57
Week, Robert P., 170–71
Wells, Arvin R., 176–77
Wells, H. G., 19
Wilson, Edmund, 191, 197–98, 205–6
Wister, Owen, 51–52, 219
Woolf, Virginia, 17, 19–20, 28, 41
Wordsworth, William, 18, 45

Young, Philip, 54, 80, 82, 86, 101–2, 106

Zen, 107